The Best of
BY THE NUMBERS

Published by The Society for American Baseball Research (SABR)
P.O. Box 93183, Cleveland, Ohio 44101

Designed by Glenn LeDoux

Printed and manufactured by The Press of Ohio
3765 Sunnybrook Road, Brimfield, Ohio 44240

ISBN #0-910137-90-0

Distributed by the University of Nebraska Press
233 North Eighth Street, Lincoln, NE 68588-0255
www.nebraskapress.unl.edu

The Best of
BY THE NUMBERS

Edited by Phil Birnbaum

with contributions by

Phil Birnbaum	Sig Mejdal
Cliff Blau	Rob Neyer
Harold Brooks	Mat Olkin
Clem Comly	Pete Palmer
Paul Depodesta	Mark Pankin
F.X. Flinn	Charlie Pavitt
Tom Hanrahan	Tom Ruane
Bill James	Ron Shandler
Keith Karcher	Jayson Stark
Dan Levitt	Rob Wood

Contents

Introduction

by Phil Birnbaum

This is a book about "sabermetrics," which is the statistical analysis of baseball. It's not obvious what "sabermetrics" means, and even "statistical analysis of baseball" is kind of vague. So the new reader might be wondering what it is we do, and what this book is about.

First, let me tell you what it's not about. It's not about compiling those batting and pitching lines that you find in agate type in the newspaper. It's not about those arcane bits of trivia you occasionally see at the bottom of the TV screen during games ("Joe is 21 for 55 against left-handed pitchers in August"). It's not even about ranking and evaluating players (although we occasionally indulge in a bit of that).

If it's not that, what is it? This: We study the available evidence to answer questions about baseball, questions that are pertinent to anyone with an interest in the game. We consider sabermetrics a science. Indeed, Craig Wright has defined sabermetrics as "scientific research of the available evidence to identify, study, and measure forces in professional baseball."

For instance, here's a question: do clutch-hitting players exist? That is, are there players who have consistently demonstrated an intrinsic ability to hit better than their usual level when the game is on the line?

That's one of the best examples of the kind of question we love to research, because every baseball fan wants to know the answer, everyone has an intuitive opinion, and the question can be answered from the evidence of the statistical record. You can see some of that evidence in Pete Palmer's study, elsewhere in this book. And the evidence suggests that clutch hitting does not appear to be a repeatable skill that a player can have.

This is perhaps an unexpected conclusion. Some fans don't accept it, and they are welcome to challenge the evidence. One of the tenets of the scientific method is that any theory must always remain vulnerable to new and contradictory evidence or reasoning. It is quite conceivable that we're just not measuring the right thing, or we didn't interpret the evidence properly. Maybe someone just made a mistake in the calculations.

But many fans, on hearing the sabermetric view, don't look at the evidence—they reflexively insist that we must be wrong. "You see," they will explain patiently, "it's part of life that some people perform better under pressure, and some worse. That must also be true in baseball." That, indeed, is what our intuition tells us. But baseball, like life, is full of the unexpected. Like any science, sabermetrics is forced to go where the evidence tells us, whether it agrees with conventional wisdom or not.

Not all of the studies in this book disprove conventional wisdom, of course—but some of them do. And if you're the type who likes to see your ideas challenged in unexpected ways, we think you'll appreciate the research in this book.

*   *   *   *

Here's another example of the kinds of questions we study: who contributed more to his team's offense in 1998: Mark McGwire, or Sammy Sosa?

One sabermetric result that casts light on this question is "Runs Created." It's one of the most famous—and elegant—formulas in Sabermetrics:

$$\text{RUNS} = \frac{(H + BB) \times (\text{TOTAL BASES})}{(AB + BB)}$$

This formula was created (or "discovered," depending on your point of view) by Bill James in the 1970s. The idea behind it is this: to score runs, you need to (a) get runners on base, (b) advance them, and (c) do all this in the fewest number of opportunities. The formula reflects this truth, being (a) multiplied by (b), divided by (c). The close relationship between the formula, and the way common sense suggest that runs are actually scored, is one of the points in its favor.

However, the elegance of the Runs Created formula isn't enough—it actually has to "work." That is, if the formula claims to predict how many runs will score, it must be judged on how well it makes that prediction, not how well it appeals to the reader. If it didn't work, we wouldn't use it.

But it does work pretty well. Take, for instance, the 2001 Seattle Mariners, whose team batting line was this:

	AB	H	2B	3B	HR	BB	AVG
2001 Mariners	5680	1637	310	38	169	614	.288

The runs created formula predicts the Mariners would have scored 905 runs. They actually scored 927. The difference, 22 runs out of 905, is typical for Runs Created. If you repeated the calculation for the rest of the 2001 AL teams, you'd find that Runs Created ranged from perfect (The Royals were predicted to score 729 runs, and they did) to less so (The A's overshot their estimate by 54 runs, 884 to 830). But it was within a creditable 2% of the actual total for about half the teams. It was also very successful in separating the better teams from the worst teams, correctly picking the top four and bottom four run-scoring teams (although not in exact order).

It is in this sense that Runs Created "works"—its prediction is usually very close to the actual number of runs. The results would be even closer if we used the more complicated versions of Runs Created, which include stolen bases, sacrifices, and other statistics that don't appear in the basic version we're using here.

If you calculated Runs Created for each player on a team, then added them up, you'd get very close to the Runs Created for the team as a whole. And so it seems reasonable to apply the formula to a single player's batting line, to compute how many runs a player "creates" for his team. Getting back to the original question, here are the famous batting lines of Mark McGwire and Sammy Sosa in 1998:

	AB	H	2B	3B	HR	BB	AVG	RC
McGwire	509	152	21	0	70	162	.299	179
Sosa	643	198	20	0	66	73	.308	157

Runs Created tells us that McGwire created 179 runs, while Sosa created "only" 157.

But comparing Runs Created between two players is complicated by the fact that that they may not have had similar playing time. In some cases, you want to compare not the total number of runs a player produced, but the rate at which he produces runs. The stat that does this (again, courtesy of Bill James) is called "RC/G," for "Runs Created per game," or sometimes "RC27," which stands for "runs created per 27 outs."

The formula is simply:

$$[RC / (AB - H)] \times 25.5$$

At-bats minus hits is just the number of outs the player consumed. And so, RC27 is simply Runs Created divided by outs, and multiplied by 25.5. (We use 25.5 instead of 27 because even though there are 27 outs per game, only 25.5 outs occur through a hitless at-bat. The rest occur through baserunner outs.)

Again comparing McGwire and Sosa:

	RC	Outs	RC27
McGwire	179	357	12.8
Sosa	157	445	9.0

You can interpret RC27 this way: if we put together a team of nine Mark McGwires, and let them play ball, they'd score an average 12.8 runs per game. They'd beat a team of nine Sammy Sosas by an average score of 13 to 9. (Actually, the correct numbers are probably closer to 12 and 8. Research has shown that Runs Created is a bit overoptimistic for extreme offenses such as a team of Sosas or McGwires. There are other offensive evaluation statistics, such as Linear Weights and Extrapolated Runs, which appear to be more accurate than Runs Created in these situations.)

Runs Created is sometimes called a "player evaluation statistic," but in reality it does not intrinsically claim to evaluate or rank players. It simply demonstrates a relationship between a batting line and the number of runs that will score. It certainly can be used in an argument that compares players, and many analysts have used it to argue that McGwire should have won the 1998 MVP instead of Sosa. But Runs Created can be used in many other ways, and for many other purposes. Some of those you will see in the studies that follow.

*　*　*　*

I have been referring to the analysts in this book as "we"—this is what "we" do, this is how "we" do it, and here's what "we" have proven. That's a bit arrogant, because, for the most part, the work of "we" authors in this book is dwarfed by the body of knowledge that preceded us.

The reality is that "we" are standing on the shoulders of the proverbial giants—most notably, Pete Palmer and Bill James.

Palmer's 1984 book, *The Hidden Game of Baseball*, is still considered the best introduction to the field of baseball statistics; he will be quoted frequently in the pages that follow.

And the work of Bill James, in his annual *Baseball Abstract* series (1977 to 1988) and subsequent projects, has provided us with more objective, analytical knowledge of baseball than any ten analysts before or since. George F. Will called James' work "the most important scientific treatise since Newton's Principia." Though this is obviously a bit of an exaggeration, it captures the sense of the intellectual achievement that is James' work.

If you find your interest sparked by the studies in this book, the works of Palmer and James are the place to start. Though long out of print, they are usually available on eBay and other internet auction sites.

*   *   *   *

With all the work that has come before, baseball research occasionally winds up a bit impenetrable to the beginner. This is true in any field, not just baseball analysis.

But don't be put off. For this compilation, we have tried to choose studies that stand well on their own. Just a bit of familiarity with the Runs Created statistic, which we described a page or two earlier, should be enough to get you through most of the essays. And, as for the mathematics—well, a certain amount of math is unavoidable. But we've made sure to include a number of less mathematical articles, and many of the others involve nothing more than simple arithmetic.

At any rate, even the most technical articles study subjects that are of interest to the casual fan, and if you skip over the heavier math, you should find the baseball issues readily comprehensible.

We can't promise that you will love everything you read here. But we can promise that from every study, you will learn new and interesting things about the game, things that serious baseball fans are interested in.

And that—not the mathematics—is the goal.

About By the Numbers

The essays in this book originally appeared over the past fifteen years in *By the Numbers*, a publication of the Society for American Baseball Research.

Published quarterly, *By the Numbers* features original and wide-ranging statistical research from members of the Statistical Analysis Committee of SABR. Though SABR counts among its members many professional writers (some of whom have generously contributed introductions to this book), most of the studies in BTN are written by contributors who do not make their living in baseball. They produce this research out of love for (or obsession with) the game.

By the Numbers is available on request to any SABR member, as a privilege of membership.

Introduction to "Catchers: Better as Veterans"

Think about a great defensive catcher. What do you think of? Probably a great arm, able to stop the running game . . . great at fielding a bunt, good at blocking the plate, effective at getting in front of an overthrown ball to prevent the wild pitch.

But what about the other aspects of the catcher's job? Perhaps because they are more subtle, they are barely noticed. What about the ability to call the right pitch? Or to handle the pitcher, patting him on the back at the right time, and knowing when and what to say to get him to pitch out of trouble? Which catchers are best at turning balls into strikes by framing the pitch?

There are no statistics for these aspects of the catcher's job, nor could there be—the art of psyching a struggling starter into finding the plate, how can you evaluate that? How can you decide how many times Mike Piazza fools the umpire into calling a strike on an inside pitch by flicking his glove just so?

But while we can't see these results directly, they do leave footprints. If a catcher handles the pitcher well, frames the strike zone, and calls the right pitch, we should see the ERA of his pitchers reduced. The better the catcher is, the better the pitcher's stats. Those we can measure.

But for the most part, we didn't. Bill James, in the early '80s, did base 10% of the catcher's defensive ratings on his staff's ERA, but how do you separate the pitchers' skill from the catcher's? Even at 10%, the ratings would be biased toward teams with better pitchers. A few years later, Pete Palmer and John Thorn, in *The Hidden Game of Baseball*, mentioned that handling the pitcher and calling the game are the catcher's "main defensive contribution," but evaluated catcher defense only in the traditional range and throwing areas.

Finally, in 1989, Craig Wright (in his book, *The Diamond Appraised*) investigated the elusive aspects of catcher defense more thoroughly. He isolated the catcher's impact on the game by comparing him, not to other teams' catchers (since other teams use other pitchers, who may be better or worse), but to his own team's backup catchers when handling the same pitchers. For instance, Wright reported that, matching up the pitchers inning for inning, the Texas Rangers staff had an ERA 41 points lower with Don Slaught behind the plate than with other catchers (4.14 vs. 4.55). But with Mike Stanley catching, the pitchers' ERAs were 38 points higher, 5.03 to 4.65.

Wright also presented the fascinating case study of Jim Sundberg. From 1977 to 1982, the staff ERA was higher with Sundberg behind the plate in every one of the six years (actually, one of the six was a tie). But starting in 1983, Rangers coach Glen Ezell worked with Sundberg on improving these aspects of his game. Over the next five and a half years, Sundberg's pitchers were 12 points better with him than with his backups, suggesting that this aspect of the backstop's game is a coachable, learnable skill. (Wright was an employee of the Rangers organization at the time, and saw all this first-hand.)

Wright's seminal study suggests the question: do catchers get better at this aspect of their game as they get older and more experienced? Wright's research suggests that they can learn—but do they learn? In this article Tom Hanrahan looks at just this question. His conclusion—well, the title of his study gives it away—is something we should have suspected, but that nobody previously predicted.

PHIL BIRNBAUM

Catchers: Better as Veterans

by Tom Hanrahan

Introduction

A catcher's main job, everyone knows, is to call a game and handle the pitching staff. Yet in a game that has statistics for virtually everything, there seems to be precious little time and energy devoted to measuring how well catchers do their main job. Rather, we see a catcher's defense measured by how many base stealers he throws out, and all of his other defensive skills ("framing" the pitch, setting up the hitter, bringing along the pitcher) are defined anecdotally by TV announcers. This study is an attempt to determine if catchers' defensive abilities as a whole improve as they mature and adjust to a pitching staff, and to quantify this as much as is possible.

We start by asking the question: What general factors might affect a catcher's ability to handle a pitching staff? I suggest that his ability might vary with:

- His age and experience
- His familiarity with the pitchers he is catching
- His familiarity with the batters his pitcher is facing

There may be other specific factors like special tutoring under a specific coach, but these kinds of things will not help us answer the question in general. Tests could be set up to measure any one of these. My aim here was to see if catchers' defense improved on the whole as they became familiar with a pitching staff. At the end of this paper, I will look at how the findings here might be broken down into their individual factors.

The Study

How do we best measure a catcher's defensive abilities? I propose the only reasonable answer is the ERA of the team for which he is catching. How could we best isolate a catcher's defensive ability from all of the other factors that cause a team ERA to rise or fall? I attempted to do this by using all of the teams that had the same *primary catcher in consecutive seasons*. I defined "primary" as having caught at least 85 games during a season. I used the years 1946-1987—beginning after the players returned from WWII and going through the last year in my baseball encyclopedia. No adjustments were made for strike years or change in length of the season. I did not use years when a team changed cities.

There were 104 catchers used in the study. The total number of catcher years was 539, representing about 60,000 total games caught. This gave me a large set of matched pairs of teams in consecutive years using the same catcher. I found the team ERA for each year and compared it to the league average. I also recorded the number of games the team's catcher had caught in his career prior to the start of the season. Obviously there was always some movement of pitchers between years, some hurlers improving or declining, changes in the team defense at other positions, and changes in ballpark dimensions. But if I could get a large enough sample that all of these other factors got washed out in the noise, I would be able to see if the number of games caught by the catcher was an important contributor to the team ERA.

As an example, I will use Bob Boone's career. He caught at least 85 games every year except the strike year of 1981:

Table 1. BOB BOONE'S CAREER

YR	TM	PREV. GC	TM. ERA	LG. ERA	DIFFERENCE FROM LEAGUE	DIFFERENCE FROM PREV. YR.	DIFFERENCE FROM 3 YRS. AGO
1973	PHI	14	4.00	3.67	+0.33		
1974	PHI	149	3.92	3.62	+0.30	-.03	
1975	PHI	295	3.82	3.63	+0.19	-.11	
1976	PHI	387	3.10	3.50	-0.40	-.59	-.73
1977	PHI	495	3.71	3.91	-0.20	+.20	-.50
1978	PHI	626	3.33	3.58	-0.25	-----	-.44
1979	PHI	755	4.16	3.73	+0.43	+.68	+.83
1980	PHI	872	3.43	3.60	-0.17	-.60	+.03
1982	CAL	1085	3.82	4.07	-0.25	-----	-----
1983	CAL	1228	4.31	4.06	+0.25	-----	-----
1984	CAL	1370	3.96	3.99	+0.03	-.22	-----
1985	CAL	1507	3.91	4.15	-0.24	-----	+.01
1986	CAL	1654	3.84	4.18	+0.34	+.58	+.09
1987	CAL	1798	4.38	4.46	+0.08	-.26	+.05

In his rookie year, with Boone having caught only 14 games prior to 1973, the team ERA was .33 runs per game higher than the league average. In his second season, this improved slightly to .30 higher than the league average, just .03 runs per game better. Substantial improvement was shown in the next two years, after which there was a meandering slow drop off until he retired. We have seven pairs of years while he was with the Phillies ('73-73, '74-75 . . . '79-80), and five pairs of years with the Angels. Even if he had caught full-time in 1981, the pair of years '80-81 would not be used in the study because he switched teams (and pitching staffs).

Organizing the Data

I built two groups of data. In the first I grouped the year-pairs in bins of hundreds of career games caught: 0-99, 100-199, etc. I used only those pairs of consecutive years where the catcher's games crossed from one to the next. Thus, we can use Boone's '73-74, but not '77-78, because he crossed right through the 500s. This grouping was used to focus on changes from one year to the next, so I could build a function over time. Controlling the number of games caught (by 100s) allowed me to use that as the variable that could link one group to the next. There were 306 matched year-pairs using this method. I think this method gives a good deal of organization to the data (it's easy to use and see the trends), but I did lose a few of the samples.

Second, I tried to compare rookies to veterans directly by comparing years that were somewhat further apart. In the next grouping, I again organized the data into hundreds bins, but this time I compared them not to the previous year, but to their record three years ago, having caught for the same team for four consecutive years. I did not control how many career games the catcher had three seasons prior. Going back to the Boone example, between 1973 and 1976 the Phillies' ERA improved relative to the league by .73 runs per game (from .33 to -.40). So, I recorded one data point for catchers with career games caught in the 300s, a team ERA of -.73 compared to three years ago. This second grouping contained fewer points, because not as many catchers started at least 85 games for the same team for this length of time. I chose three years as the comparison point because the more years apart, the less data there is, so using a longer time span would be difficult, and the results of the first data grouping suggested that a three-year span would show noticeable differences.

After trying this three-year comparison, I wound up focusing exclusively on comparing raw rookies to veterans, since this is where the most obvious differences appeared.

Comparing Consecutive Seasons (Grouping One)

I found 49 consecutive year-pairs where the catcher's career games caught went from 99 or less to between 100-199. The average team had an ERA .07 runs per game lower when the catchers had the extra year (= 100 games) of experience. Table 2 shows the data from every bin. As the amount of data became small for catchers with over 1,000 games, I combined the last groups to ensure my sample sizes were at least 15.

The data in Table 2 strongly suggest that the catchers' defensive ability improves steadily until they have caught somewhere between 400 and 800 games with the same club in the major leagues. The team ERA drops about three-tenths of a run per game from the time they have their first full season until they reach this level of maturity. After this there is a slow rise in the team ERA until the catcher retires.

The right-most column of Table 2, cumulative difference, is plotted as Chart 1. The bars show the standard deviation of the cumulated difference in ERA from year 1 through the year plotted.

Table 2. EFFECTS OF EXPERIENCE ON CATCHER ERA

CAREER GC BETW. 2 YRS.	# SAMPLES (YEAR-PAIRS)	AVERAGE ERA DIFFERENCE	SDEV OF ERA DIFFERENCES	CUMULATIVE ERA DIFFERENCE	
000s–100s	49	-.07	.40	-.07	
100s–200s	44	-.02	.43	-.09	
200s–300s	39	-.12	.40	-.21	
300s–400s	29	-.04	.37	-.25	
400s–500s	25	-.02	.36	-.27	
500s–600s	28	-.02	.36	-.29	
600s–700s	22	.00	.34	-.29	
700s–800s	20	+.06	.34	-.23	
800s–900s	15	+.04	.25	-.19	
900s–1000s & 1000s–1100s	19	+.08/year	.37	-.11 (1000s)	-.03 (1100s)
1100s–1200s thru 1600s–1700s	16	+.11/year*	.27	†	

* Very limited sample

† Sample too small for six-year projection

Chart 1. CUMULATIVE ERA DIFFERENCES BY CATCHER EXPERIENCE

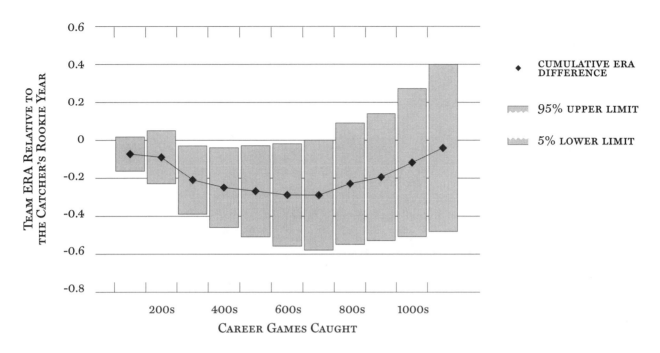

Standard Deviation (SDEV)

The variation (or "noise") in measuring ERAs from year to year is measured by the SDEV (column 4). This typically was about .35 to .40 runs per game. We can use this to measure how certain we are that the average ERA difference is not just a random happening, assuming the data is normally distributed, which seems to be a reasonable assumption in this instance. In the first row, the average ERA difference is -.07, and is based on 49 samples. The SDEV *of the average* is found by dividing the sample SDEV by the square root of the number of samples; in this case:

$$\frac{40}{\sqrt{49}} = .06$$

So, the average ERA difference is -.07, plus or minus .06. We can create a "confidence level" that states that the average ERA difference is between -.13 and -.01 with 68% certainty, or between -.17 and .05 (plus or minus two standard deviations) with 95% certainty. If we wanted to compare Row 1 with Row 5 (and we certainly do), by adding the effects we see the cumulative ERA difference is -.30. The SDEV of the cumulative difference is found to be .15 by taking the root sum square of each row's SDEV of the average. Thus, the difference in team ERA between the catchers with less than 100 games caught and those with 400-500 games caught is probably (68% certainly) between −.45 and −.15, according to this set of data. This means that we are not entirely sure that this effect is real, or how large it is, just from this set of data organized in this manner.

Comparisons Over Three Years (Grouping Two)

Table 3 shows the catcher year-pairs organized by 100s bins in a different manner. The 279-300s row shows that there were 14 catchers we could use to compare the team ERA between the year when they had between 279-399 games caught under their belts to the team ERA three years prior to that. The average number of games caught in each career three years prior is shown. The first row indicates that after three years, the team ERA averaged .28 runs per game lower. It also shows that of the 14 teams represented, 12 of the 14 had a lower team ERA (relative to the league average) when the catcher was a veteran of 279-399 games, as compared to three years prior when he had caught only an average of 27 games in his career.

Table 3. EFFECT ON ERA WITH GAMES CAUGHT

CAREER GC ENTERING LATTER YR.	AVG. CG 3 YRS. PRIOR	# SAMPLES (YEAR-PAIRS)	AVG. ERA DIFFERENCES	# OF TEAMS WITH LOWER/HIGHER ERA
279*-300s	27	14	-.28	12/02
400s	82	24	-.38	20/04
500s	172	33	-.15	23/10
600s	+/- 280	26	-.10	16/10
700s	+/- 380	22	+.04	08/14
800s	+/- 480	19	+.16	06/13
900s–1000s	+/- 630	24	-.02	12/12
1100s–1700s	350 fewer	28	+.07	11/17

*279 was the minimum number of career games caught for any catcher who also was a starting catcher 3 years ago.

The data in Table 3 is pretty much in agreement with that in Table 2—significant improvement in team ERA the first few years, and a slow decrease in performance toward the catcher's later years. The item that jumped right out at me was the first two rows of the right-hand column. In those rows, out of 38 teams, 32 of them had ERAs that were lower with the catchers who had an extra three years of experience. With all of the changes that likely occurred in the team pitching staffs and other defensive changes over the years, it strikes me as remarkable that about 85% of the teams would improve their pitching.

As I studied the 38 catcher seasons involved here, I noticed that the trend was even stronger when using just the catchers who had virtually no previous major league experience. So I organized the data one last time, using *only* catchers who had *very* little experience (less than 50 games) prior to their first full-time year, and making comparison to their "prime" years. Table 2 showed that the catchers' prime seemed to be when he had caught between 400 and 799 games (this is where the cumulative ERA was the lowest). I found all catchers who

a) caught at least 85 games in a season, having had 50 or less career games coming into that year, and

b) caught at least 85 games in other seasons, with the same team, having 400-799 career games caught before these other seasons.

There were 16 comparisons. The teams, "rookie" years and catchers used were:

NATIONAL			AMERICAN		
LA	1958	Roseboro	Bos	1952	White
Phi	1961	Dalrymple	Bal	1956	Triandos
SF	1962	Haller	Was	1966	Casanova
StL	1963	McCarver	Chi	1969	Hermann
Chi	1966	Hundley	NY	1970	Munson
Cin	1968	Bench	Bos	1972	Fisk
Pit	1969	Sanguillen	Tex	1974	Sundberg
Phi	1973	Boone	Min	1976	Wynegar

I recorded the team ERA (relative to the league) in the rookie year and the average team ERA of all years used in the "prime veteran" classification. Of the 16 teams, only *one* had their ERA get worse when the catcher went from rookie to veteran status; fifteen teams had better ERAs with the veteran catchers. The average improvement was .47 runs per game, or 76 runs over a 162-game season! This is very likely a larger difference than importing Ozzie Smith, Willie Mays, or Bill Mazeroski in their primes to help

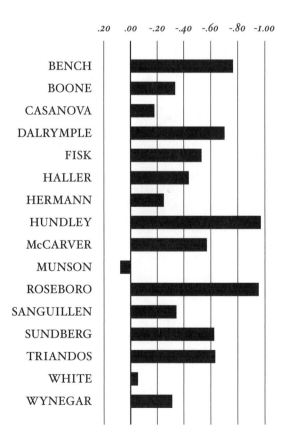

your defense. It's even more remarkable when you consider that the ERA comparisons are for the whole season, including the games these catchers did *not* start. Many of these catchers caught three-fourths or less of their teams' games, so the improvement per game caught might be 30-40% more! The data for these 16 teams and catchers are graphed in the chart below.

I went back and checked to see what each of these 16 teams' ERA was in the year *prior* to these catchers being rookies, just to make sure that what I was seeing here wasn't some strange effect, such as a group of all-world defensive catchers (there *were* some mighty fine names in this bunch) helping their teams tremendously while they were in their peak years. Well, these teams were *worse* than the league by an average of .22 earned runs per game in the year that they were full-time rookies (the years given above in the list). In other words, in their first year these catchers appeared to hurt their team defensively by a fifth to a quarter of a run per game. Then, over the next two to five years, their defensive skills improved enough to help their team ERA go down by almost a half run a game, so there was some net improvement comparing their prime years to the year before they showed up.

One of the teams in this study was the '58 Dodgers, who moved into a vastly better pitchers' park in 1962, so we shouldn't be surprised that the team ERA improved so much with Roseboro catching as he became a veteran. Still, tossing out one data point won't make that much difference.

Objections

Maybe the sample is too small and we're seeing some random effects.
Overruled. Already covered this; there's too much data here, especially when 15 of the 16 teams improve over time . . . If you flip 16 coins, 15 of them will come up heads less than one time in 3,800.

What if the catchers represented an anomalous group of some kind?
In the second grouping (comparisons over three years), obviously catchers who washed out of the majors didn't factor in, since they never reached veteran status. So one could argue that maybe these were the catchers who *did* learn how to call a game, and the others did not. But in the first grouping, we used consecutive year-pairs across every level of games caught, and the same pattern was evident. Overruled again.

Park factors? Moving over time to a pitching-dominated era?
We compared everything relative to the league and within the same teams to get rid of park and trend effects. These guys were good catchers on good teams, so which came first, the chicken or the egg?

Conclusions

A typical catcher handles a pitching staff better and better during his first few years in the majors with a club. This is evident by the rather dramatic drop in the team ERA of about a third of a run per game from his rookie season to his prime years with a club.

If you have a veteran catcher who has been with your team for some time, and you're thinking of trading him and calling up the young phenom from AAA, you can expect your pitching results to get worse. Of course, you ought to call him up *sometime*, but don't expect the team to improve right away. How many catchers are offensively 50 runs a year better than their replacement? (Piazza begins and ends the short list.)

The differences in catchers' stolen bases allowed are apparently *less* important than their other defensive abilities. The worst-throwing catchers in the majors do not allow anywhere near one stolen base per game more than Ivan Rodriguez does.

———

This article originally appeared in the August 1999 issue of *By The Numbers*.

On-Base Plus Slugging

In general, few of the sabermetric research findings of the past couple of decades have made it into popular use. Pick up your newspaper and you'll find little mention of Runs Created or Pythagorean Projection, for instance.

But one sabermetric finding that has made a slight bit of headway and garnered a bit of acceptance in mainstream baseball is "OPS." Peter Gammons mentions it occasionally, and MLB.com includes it in batters' statistical lines.

OPS simply stands for "On-base percentage plus slugging percentage." It's a quick-and-dirty measure of a player's offensive contribution. It's quick because there's no fancy formula—you just add up the SLG and OBP columns from the official stats. It's dirty because it's a rough estimate of offensive contribution. Runs Created and Linear Weights, to name two, are more accurate.

But while other stats work better, OPS is still a good measure. Research shows that it correlates well, in most cases, with its more accurate sister stats. There is no better statistic that's so easy to compute.

Here is how OPS assesses the 1998 McGwire and Sosa seasons:

	AB	H	2B	3B	HR	BB	AVG	OBP	SLG	OPS
McGwire	509	152	21	0	70	162	.299	.470	.752	1.222
Sosa	643	198	20	0	66	73	.308	.377	.647	1.024

McGwire's OPS advantage—almost 200 points—is huge. So huge, in fact, that despite OPS's imperfect assessment, we are still fairly safe in concluding that McGwire was more productive than Sosa that season.

Introduction to "Stolen Base Strategies Revisited"

A good way to start an argument is to bring up the value of the stolen base as a tactical weapon. An adherent of traditional wisdom might throw out some phrases like "putting pressure on the defense" and "manufacturing runs," and might throw in a Maury Wills anecdote for good measure. An analyst might be unpersuaded, but his or her objections likely would tend toward the theoretical—the high cost of a runner caught stealing versus the relatively modest pay-off, the advancement of a single base. The debate has raged for years, due in no small part to a lack of hard evidence on the issue.

One of the first works that provided something beyond mere anecdotes and authoritative proclamations was Earnshaw Cook's *Percentage Baseball* in 1964. Using a decade's worth of actual major league data, Cook concluded that in order to make a positive contribution, a base stealer needed to steal successfully in roughly two-thirds of his attempts. This so-called "break-even point" was determined to be somewhat lower in two-out situations.

Pete Palmer seconded Cook's conclusions in *The Hidden Game of Baseball* in 1984. Based on the results of computer simulations of over eighty years' worth of major league games, Palmer created a table of "scoring probabilities" for all the base-out situations (e.g., runners at the corners and one out). He agreed that a two-thirds success rate generally was needed in order to yield an increase in scoring.

Such conclusions were more helpful to the anti-running game argument, since few running teams exceed the break-even point by a significant amount in a given season. With respect to the steal's overall impact as an offensive weapon, Palmer was unequivocal, calling it "at best a dubious method of increasing a team's run production."

Many agreed with Palmer's conclusion. Others, though, raised quite reasonable objections; one was that the so-called break-even rate was only an average, and thus did not apply equally to all players in all situations.

This is one of several issues Tom Ruane addresses in the following essay.

Using a decade's worth of major league game data, Ruane paralleled Cook and Palmer's method of analysis. Instead of simply looking for an overall break-even point, though, he focused on how the break-even point—i.e., the advisability of sending the runner—was affected by the game situation and the player's skills involved.

In doing so, he addressed long-running objections such as: stealing might decrease scoring overall. But what if you're playing for only one run? What if there are two outs? What if there's a weak hitter at the plate? How does the speed of the runner affect the equation?

Ruane's conclusions did not come down wholly on one side or the other—perhaps to the delight of those on both sides of the debate. He confirmed each side's points, in part. In doing so, he helped to move the discussion forward a bit—something that's been regrettably uncommon on this particular topic.

MAT OLKIN

Stolen Base Strategies Revisited

by Tom Ruane

In *The Hidden Game of Baseball*, Pete Palmer determined the expected future runs (EFR) for each of the 24 game situations (with outs going from 0 to 2 and bases ranging from empty to full) and used that to evaluate, among other things, break-even points for stolen base attempts. Pete used the results of computer-simulated baseball games to develop his charts. Thanks to the folks at Retrosheet and Project Scoresheet, I've been able to use actual play-by-play data to generate similar information for National Leagues games from 1980 to 1989:

MEN ON	NUMBER OF OUTS			MEN ON	NUMBER OF OUTS		
F S T	0	1	2	F S T	0	1	2
- - -	.452	.239	.091	- - -	.261	.148	.061
x - -	.815	.486	.210	x - -	.424	.267	.124
- x -	1.051	.653	.313	- x -	.608	.400	.216
xx -	1.384	.852	.404	xx -	.617	.413	.219
- - x	1.278	.912	.358	- - x	.819	.651	.269
x - x	1.638	1.131	.471	x - x	.843	.646	.275
- xx	1.884	1.313	.576	- xx	.841	.667	.274
xxx	2.176	1.481	.718	xxx	.855	.664	.316

The figures on the left are the average number of runs scored during the rest of the inning starting from the given situation. For example, in innings where the team at bat has a man on second with no one out, they add an average of 1.051 runs before making the third out. The figures on the right contain the percentage of times the team will score at least one run.

To paraphrase part of Pete's argument, since an attempt to steal second with no outs risks a loss of .576 runs (.815−.239) for a gain of .236 runs (1.051−.815), it must be successful more than 70.9% of the time to increase a team's expected runs. His formula for determining this was:

$$\frac{(\text{START EFR}-\text{FAIL EFR})}{(\text{START EFR}-\text{FAIL EFR}) + (\text{SUCCESS EFR}-\text{START EFR})}$$

or more simply:

$$\frac{(\text{START EFR}-\text{FAIL EFR})}{(\text{SUCCESS EFR}-\text{FAIL EFR})}$$

Palmer's study was more complicated than I've suggested here, using tables like these in conjunction with others containing win probabilities for various game situations (bottom of the seventh, home team down by a run), and like much of that book, it represented a major advancement in the analysis of the game. But while it has been used as a foundation for several other studies, it has also come in for its share of criticism. One of the major criticisms is that it ignores the varying abilities of the players involved. How different would the chart above be if the hitters due up were Ruth and Gehrig? Or Rey Ordonez and Bobby Jones? What if Rickey Henderson were the lead runner? Or Ernie Lombardi? Another criticism is that Palmer's study treats the stolen base as a binary event, when in fact, it has several possible outcomes.

Despite the general title, in this article we'll be looking at the wisdom of attempting to steal second with only first base occupied. The main reason for this is that it's far and away the most common base-running situation. In 1987, for example, it accounted for 77.7% of all stolen base activity. An attempted steal of second base with men on first and third was a distant runner-up with 9.1%. But while I'll be limiting my discussion to one class of stolen base, I will be including data that will allow the reader to apply the same method to the other scenarios.

Here are the break-even points for a steal of second using Pete Palmer's formula:

NUMBER OF OUTS:	0	1	2
BREAK-EVEN PCT:	70.9	70.4	67.1

In general, Palmer tended to downplay the dangers of an aggressive running game, which is ironic in light what he said in his book:

The stolen base . . . is an overrated play, with even the best base stealers contributing few extra runs or wins to their teams. The reason for this is that the break-even point is so high, roughly two steals in three attempts.

One of the problems with this kind of analysis is that there's already some amount of stealing and getting caught already embedded in the data, perhaps skewing the results. This is perhaps more easily seen by example. I arrived at the 70.9 in the table above by plugging the following numbers into the break-even formula:

$$(.815 - .239) / (1.051 - .239)$$

But what if every time a runner was on first in this situation, he successfully stole second? In that case the expected runs from the starting state (man on first, no one out) would equal the expected runs from the "success" state (man on second, no one out), since whenever we hit the first we made a successful transition to the second. This would have modified the above formula to:

$$(1.051 - .239) / (1.051 - .239)$$

making it appear as if there were nothing to be gained by attempting to steal second. Conversely, if the runner took off and was caught each time, the formula would've been transformed into:

$$(.239 - .239) / (1.051 - .239)$$

making it appear as if there were no risk involved. One way to attempt to correct for this is to remove the type of plays being evaluated from the charts. How is this done? I generated the original charts by examining every play, determining the starting situation (outs and baserunners) and calculating the number of runs scored from that play until the end of the inning. To remove stolen base events (and here I'm including stolen bases, caught stealing, pickoffs, errors attempting pickoffs, and balks), I simply ignore any of these plays when generating the charts. Consider the following inning:

OUTS	MEN ON	RUNS	PLAY
0	- - -	2	STRIKEOUT
1	- - -	2	WALK
1	F - -	2	STEAL OF SECOND
1	- S -	2	WALK
1	F S -	2	CAUGHT STEALING THIRD, TRAILING RUNNER TO SECOND
2	- S -	2	TWO-RUN HOME RUN
2	- - -	0	STRIKEOUT

When determining the expected future runs at the start of this section, I included the data for all of these plays. To remove stolen base events from the chart, I would not factor in the two running plays above. Note that this doesn't prevent these plays from affecting the data. For example, in the inning above I would record that two runs were scored from the no one on/none out situation. But clearly that result was affected by both the steal of second (which may have caused the subsequent walk) and the caught stealing.

Here's what the adjusted chart looks like:

OUTCOMES WHEN A STEAL WAS NOT ATTEMPTED ON THE NEXT PLAY

MEN ON	NUMBER OF OUTS			MEN ON	NUMBER OF OUTS		
FST	0	1	2	FST	0	1	2
- - -	.452	.239	.091	- - -	.261	.148	.061
x - -	.816	.489	.206	x - -	.415	.262	.118
-x-	1.052	.650	.313	-x-	.608	.397	.216
xx-	1.395	.855	.404	xx-	.618	.414	.219
- -x	1.281	.922	.357	- -x	.821	.658	.267
x-x	1.643	1.142	.464	x-x	.848	.658	.271
-xx	1.886	1.315	.574	-xx	.841	.668	.271
xxx	2.177	1.484	.716	xxx	.856	.666	.314

The before and after break-even points:

	RUNNING			WITHOUT RUNNING		
NUMBER OF OUTS	0	1	2	0	1	2
BREAK-EVEN PCT	70.9	70.4	67.1	71.0	71.1	65.8

So those earlier percentages were slightly lower with none and one out and a little too high with two outs. But it doesn't appear as if the running plays affected the data much at all.

Given these break-even points, has all that baserunning helped or hindered the team at bat? One way to look at this is to generate charts using only those events removed earlier and then compare the two sets.

OUTCOMES WHEN A STEAL WAS ATTEMPTED ON THE NEXT PLAY

MEN ON	NUMBER OF OUTS			MEN ON	NUMBER OF OUTS		
FST	0	1	2	FST	0	1	2
x--	.811	.475	.237	x--	.468	.293	.161
-x-	1.031	.723	.330	-x-	.628	.481	.239
xx-	1.114	.776	.437	xx-	.589	.404	.230
--x	.533	.340	.588	--x	.467	.284	.559
x-x	1.643	1.033	.548	x-x	.794	.546	.322
-xx	1.584	.929	.911	-xx	.889	.500	.667
xxx	2.000	1.042	1.222	xxx	.727	.458	.815

The differences with a man on first:

	RUNS			PROB. OF SCORING		
NUMBER OF OUTS	0	1	2	0	1	2
DIFF. WHEN RUNNING	-.005	-.014	+.031	+.053	+.031	+.043

The -.014 in the second column means that teams scored an average of .014 fewer runs when, with a man on first and one out, the runner attempted to steal second than they did when the man on first didn't run. These differences aren't much, but they do seem to indicate that running is a much better strategy either with two outs or as part of a one-run strategy than it is otherwise.

But how does the speed of the lead runner change this? No one disputes that Will Clark (who was caught on 17 of his 22 attempts in 1987) should have run less than he did, but what about Tim Raines and Vince Coleman?

Using the Speed Score statistic devised by Bill James in his 1987 *Baseball Abstract*, I grouped the lead runners into three categories, using scores of 3.0 and 5.5 as the dividing lines*. When I initially looked at this, I found something very surprising: the speed of the lead runner was almost as important as the ability of the subsequent batters in determining the number of runs scored during the rest of the inning. And that brings us to the second trap inherent in this type of study: always be sure to isolate what you want to examine. What I had been doing originally was compounding the effects of skilled batters *and* fast runners. In other words, when fast runners are on base (for example, a typical lead-off hitter), the batters coming up are generally better than those at the plate when slow runners are aboard. So while I thought I was examining the speed of the lead runner, I was also letting the effects of a better class of hitter leach into my study. So I changed the test to ignore all cases where the weighted OPS (on-base plus slugging percentage) of the batters coming to the plate was less than .700 or greater than .800. This cut the sample size roughly in half, but allowed me to more closely examine the influence of speed on an offense.†

* When runners were on first and third, the speed factor of the man on first was used.

† This same problem could have skewed my previous comparison between the expected runs of stolen base events and all others. But since fast runners tend to be on ahead of better hitters, this skewing would make the conclusions even more unfavorable to the running game.

The results with a man on first base:

SPEED SCORE	NUMBER OF OUTS			NUMBER OF OUTS			AVG. OPS
	0	1	2	0	1	2	
< 3.0	.845	.484	.213	.409	.242	.120	.742
> 3.0 AND < 5.5	.837	.522	.231	.427	.283	.135	.746
> 5.5	.962	.590	.267	.497	.328	.163	.751

Despite what I said earlier about the effects of the running game, there seems to be a substantial benefit to having speed on the basepaths.

The number of expected runs increased by an average of 14% from the slow to the fast group and the chance of scoring a single run rose by 22%. Part of this is due to slightly better hitters coming to the plate. Even though we eliminated all situations where the weighted OPS of the hitters due up was less than 700 or over 800, the hitters up with fast lead runners were still slightly better.

But how much of this is due to stolen bases? What net gain or loss do we see from base-running events when we look at situations involving the fastest runners?

	STEALING			WITHOUT STEALING		
NUMBER OF OUTS	0	1	2	0	1	2
FASTEST RUNNERS	-.014	-.045	+.030	+.060	+.018	+.047
ALL RUNNERS	-.005	-.014	+.031	+.053	+.031	+.043

In this light, attempting to steal seems an even more costly strategy with the fastest runners in the lead. But we just showed that teams score more runs with speed on the basepaths—if the fast runners aren't helping their teams by stealing bases, where are those extra runs coming from? Here's what happens with a batter hits a single with a runner on first and no outs:

NO OUTS	BAT->1ST RUN->2ND	BAT->1ST RUN->3RD	BAT->2ND RUN->3RD	BAT->1ST RUN->OUT	BAT->2ND RUN->OUT	OTHER
SLOW	76.9	18.3	3.0	.4	.4	1.0
AVERAGE	66.3	28.4	2.7	.9	.7	.9
FAST	55.8	39.1	2.1	.6	.6	1.7

This is a significant improvement, especially in light of the low risk involved. The results with one and two outs are very similar.

When there's a groundout with no outs, here's what happens:

		FORCE PLAY		
	GDP	AT 2ND	AT 1ST	OTHER
SLOW	43.5	39.4	16.7	.5
AVERAGE	43.9	32.6	22.5	.9
FAST	36.0	31.2	31.3	1.5

With one out:

		FORCE PLAY		
	GDP	AT 2ND	AT 1ST	OTHER
SLOW	45.2	33.6	20.5	.7
AVERAGE	45.3	28.4	25.5	.7
FAST	42.3	27.4	29.4	.8

Again, another improvement without the extra risk of losing a baserunner. By the way, one thing I did not find with a fast runner on first was an increased number of wild pitches, passed balls, or errors.

But does speed on the base paths help the batter as well? You often hear that pitchers are distracted by the runner or will throw an inordinate proportion of fastballs, improving the performance of the batter. Is there any truth to this? Listed below are the OPSs of hitters with a man on first along with their overall OPS:*

	0 OUT		1 OUT		2 OUTS	
	1ST	OVERALL	1ST	OVERALL	1ST	OVERALL
SLOW	.765	.745	.768	.745	.727	.746
AVERAGE	.795	.746	.787	.745	.738	.746
FAST	.824	.747	.811	.749	.787	.749
TOTAL	.796	.746	.789	.747	.729	.747

So there does seem to be something tangible to this rumored benefit after all.

Finally, what should the effect of the batters' ability be on stolen base strategies? To determine this, I took a weighted average of the OPS of the next three hitters and separated them into three categories, using .700 and .800 as the dividing lines.† Since I wanted to examine stolen bases, I removed them from the study (using the method described earlier), and computed the break-even points with each class of hitter.

	NUMBER OF OUTS			NUMBER OF OUTS		
	0	1	2	0	1	2
OPS < .700	.720	.753	.627	.569	.626	.492
.700 < OPS < .800	.762	.744	.709	.604	.621	.584
OPS > .800	.792	.793	.710	.645	.661	.598

In other words, the better the hitter at the plate, the less you should run.

In *The Hidden Game of Baseball*, John Thorn and Pete Palmer entitled the chapter that discussed these strategies "The Book . . . and the Computer." Back in 1985, when their book was first published, the computer was primarily used for generating thousands of simulated games and analyzing the results. This article has been an attempt to extend their research using a computer and ten seasons of actual play-by-play data. There are several potential traps in using the methods I've employed above. Some I've pointed out to the reader and avoided; others, no doubt, I've stumbled into unwittingly. It was not my hope to have the last word on this area of baseball strategy. Rather, I've attempted to move the discussion forward and to suggest new ways to take advantage of the enormous amount of information now available to researchers in this field.

* Once again, hitters with OPSs less than .700 or greater than .800 are removed from the chart.

† The weighted OPS average was computed as follows, where OPS1, OPS2 and OPS3 represent the OPS of the man up, on deck, and the man following him, respectively: 0 out: (OPS1+OPS2+OPS3) / 3
$$1 \text{ out: } (OPS1+OPS2+(OPS3 \times .67)) / 2.67$$
$$2 \text{ out: } (OPS1 + (OPS2 \times .33)) / 1.33$$

This article originally appeared in the February 1999 issue of *By The Numbers*.

Introduction to "The Run Value of a Ball and Strike"

When I was a kid, I enjoyed taking apart common household items to see how they worked. I remember the first umbrella I disassembled; then I graduated to clocks and radios. I was never content to just enjoy things for what they were. I had to break everything down to its smallest component parts. It was the path to revelation.

Later, Bill James became my idol. Pete Palmer's *The Hidden Game of Baseball* had a permanent spot on my nightstand. They liked taking things apart, too. We had a kinship.

"He's a .300 hitter. He's good. Let it be." I remember that comment from a fellow owner in one of my first fantasy leagues. He was one of the thousands of casual fans content to just play this stupid game, never interested in looking beyond the obvious. "He never batted .300 before. He swings at everything, makes poor contact and never walks," I responded. "He's not going to hit .300 again."

But I needed proof. So I started taking things apart again.

I called it "component skills analysis." I became one of the legions of intelligent fans that realized the power of evaluating basic raw skills. We reveled in the relationships of simple events like strikeouts, walks and at-bats, and their correlations to our heralded batting average. While many viewed us fantasy geeks as a bane to intelligent analysis, I realized that if I approached these contests as statistical and economic game models, I could leverage my sabermetric learnings . . . into winnings.

Mercenary, me? Nah. I just gotta pay my mortgage.

Which is why I was blown away by the possibility of breaking down player performance into an even smaller component part. For if strikeouts and walks are revealing, imagine what we could learn from *their* components—balls and strikes! It's the fundamental difference between the Randy Johnsons and Kirk Rueters. It helps us understand the impact of the Bobby Abreus (4.3 pitches per plate appearance) versus the Randall Simons (2.7).

And now we can also answer questions like:

"What is the real value of that extra strike?"

"If every batter on a team was spotted a 3-0 count, how many runs, on average, would the team score?"

"How much impact can a catcher wield if he is able to frame pitches so that the umpire is more likely to call strikes?"

The answers will astound you.

For me, it will help my decisions regarding whether or not Brandon Duckworth deserves a spot on my fantasy roster next year. He had a poor 5.41 ERA but sported excellent peripheral stats. He was also one of the league leaders in pitches per plate appearance (4.0). How many additional strike calls per game would it take to potentially bring his ERA down into more acceptable territory? That answer is here, too.

There is great power in the small components, for they are the foundation upon which mighty dynasties are built. And that's the magic of Phil Birnbaum's findings.

Oh, and Jeffrey Leonard never did hit .300 again.

Ron Shandler

The Run Value of a Ball and Strike

by Phil Birnbaum

In studies on catcher ERA that I've seen, the authors conclude that the catcher's pitch handling can affect the pitcher's ERA by as much as half a run in either direction. That is, a pitcher whose "natural" ERA is 4.00 can rise to as much as 4.50 with a poor catcher, or drop to 3.50 with a very good catcher.

It seems to me that there are three ways a catcher can influence a pitcher's effectiveness: (a) by calling the right pitches for the pitcher's "stuff"; (b) by calling the right pitches to take advantage of the batter's weaknesses; or (c) by framing the pitch so that the umpire is more likely to call it a strike.

Thinking about this, I started to wonder about how much effect (c) could actually have. How many runs are saved if a ball is called a strike? Could the catcher's skill in this regard actually save half a run a game?

Results by Count

To find out, I ran a quick study of play-by-play data in the 1988 American League. Using Project Scoresheet data, I identified every plate appearance in which a particular count occurred. Then I computed the average linear weight run value based on the outcome of those plate appearances.

For instance, if a 2-0 count occurred three times (it actually occurred 9,114 times, but let's keep the example simple), and the eventual results were a single (linear weight .465), double (linear weight .775), and strikeout (linear weight -.273), the value of the 2-0 count would be .322 runs, the average of the three weights.

In reality, the value of the 2-0 count was .083 runs. Here's the entire set of results:

	0 STRIKES	1 STRIKE	2 STRIKES	3 STRIKES
0 BALLS	.0000	-.0365	-.0874	-.2736
1 BALL	.0288	-.0119	-.0680	-.2734
2 BALLS	.0829	.0290	-.0306	-.2732
3 BALLS	.1858	.1252	.0578	-.2733
4 BALLS	.3137	.3137	.3135	

The numbers in the table are denominated in incremental runs—that is, the difference in expected runs vs. starting that plate appearance over at 0-0.*

A couple of quick notes about the table:

The "3 strikes" column is -.2733 because that's the value of a strikeout. The "4 balls" row is .3137 because that's the value of a unintentional walk. The values vary slightly because of errors in the data (for instance, there were three instances where the Project Scoresheet file included four strikes).

The "even" counts 1-1 and 2-2 favor the pitcher. This makes sense, because both counts are closer to a strikeout (which requires only three strikes) than a walk (which requires four balls).

* Technical details: (a) I used linear weight values I calculated myself from the 1988 American League. Using the standard Pete Palmer's weights would make the results vary only slightly. (b) A plate appearance was included in the stat line for any count it passed through. So an at-bat that went ball/strike/strike/home run would have the homer included in the 0-0, 1-0, 1-1, and 1-2 stat lines. (c) Since linear weights is defined to make the average event zero, the 0-0 count must work out to zero, since every at-bat passes through that count. (d) Any situation in which an intentional ball was thrown was ignored.

Unsurprisingly, the best count for a pitcher is 0-2. The surprise is that it takes three of those 0-2 counts to save as many runs as one strikeout. On the other hand, a 3-0 count is more than half as good as a full-fledged walk.

	AB	H	2B	3B	HR	BB	K	AVG	SLG	RC27	Record
0 AND 0	77007	19965	3556	425	1901	7190	12322	.259	.391	4.34	81- 81
0 AND 1	33524	7780	1295	157	633	1627	8001	.232	.337	2.99	52-110
0 AND 2	12302	2189	348	39	161	382	4942	.178	.252	1.58	19-143
0 AND 3	2211	0	0	0	0	0	2211	.000	.000	0.00	0-162
1 AND 0	31011	8279	1546	194	896	5076	4210	.267	.416	5.36	98- 64
1 AND 1	28699	6929	1225	139	687	2581	6177	.241	.366	3.74	69- 93
1 AND 2	18874	3570	580	71	298	1050	7131	.189	.275	2.00	28-134
1 AND 3	4374	0	0	0	0	0	4371	.000	.000	0.00	0-162
2 AND 0	9114	2518	484	75	298	3707	1085	.276	.444	7.59	122- 40
2 AND 1	14260	3611	678	75	394	2935	2603	.253	.394	5.12	94- 68
2 AND 2	14171	2886	516	59	265	1856	4852	.204	.304	2.88	50-112
2 AND 3	3577	2	0	0	0	0	3575	.001	.001	0.00	0-162
3 AND 0	1546	405	63	22	55	2630	189	.262	.438	11.00	140- 22
3 AND 1	4304	1171	206	44	153	3105	610	.272	.447	9.04	132- 30
3 AND 2	6210	1389	256	37	154	2781	1840	.224	.351	5.35	98- 64
3 AND 3	1828	0	0	0	0	0	1828	.000	.000	0.00	0-162
4 AND 0	0	0	0	0	0	1573	0	.000	.000	0.00	
4 AND 1	0	0	0	0	0	2135	0	.000	.000	0.00	
4 AND 2	1	0	0	0	0	2742	0	.000	.000	0.00	
4 AND 3	0	0	0	0	0	0	0	.000	.000	0.00	

Here's the data in another form: a batting line for each of the counts. The RC27 column is Runs Created per 27 outs (25.5 batting outs), and the last column is the record of a team who scored that many runs and gave up the league average 4.34.*

With every batter spotted a 3-0 count, the average team would score 11 runs a game on their way to a 140-22 record. With every pitcher getting ahead of the count 0-2, the team would score only 1.58 runs per game, and lose 143 games per season.

More interesting, of course, are the less extreme cases. If every pitcher threw one extra strike per batter, on the first pitch, its team would win 110 games. And throwing one extra first-pitch ball, falling behind 1-0 on every batter, would reduce an average team to a 64-98 team.

*Using Pythagorean Projection with exponent 2.

Strike Value

So how much is a strike worth? The first answer is that it all depends on the count. If a 1-0 count is worth .0288 runs, and a 1-1 count is worth −0.119 runs, the strike has saved the pitcher .0407 runs—about one twenty-fifth of a run.

A strike on 3-2, however, turns a .0578 run situation into a strikeout at -.2733, a difference of a third of a run.

The 3-2 strike is the highest-valued strike in the table, worth about nine (!) first-pitch strikes. The old saw has that the best pitch in baseball is strike one, but, clearly, the best pitch in baseball is actually strike three.

So not all strikes are created equal, nor all balls. But we can easily get an *average* value for strikes and balls. Again for the entire league, I calculated the run reduction for all the strikes and balls and averaged them. (This average is weighted by count frequency, because an 0-0 strike happens much more often than an 0-2 strike.)

The result:

A STRIKE IS WORTH −0.0829 RUNS.
A BALL IS WORTH +0.0560 RUNS.

Surprisingly, or perhaps not, a strike is worth about 1/3 of the value of a strikeout, and a ball is worth close to 1/4 the value of a walk (actually, a bit less).

The Catcher

If a catcher is successful in framing a ball so that the umpire calls it a strike, the defensive team saves the difference between the two values:

TURNING A BALL INTO A STRIKE SAVES .1389 RUNS, OR ABOUT 1/7 OF A RUN.

So, does it seem reasonable that a difference of half a run per game can be obtained just by framing pitches better? Well, 0.5 runs per game is about four extra balls turned into strikes—four more than an average catcher. Does that seem plausible? I don't really watch enough games, or pay enough attention to pitch framing, to answer that question. But my intuition would suggest that one or two pitches seems reasonable.

One pitch a game better than average is about 20 runs a season. That's two extra games in the win column, or about a third to a half the added value of a superstar free agent. It can be as big a consideration as the catcher's batting line and throwing arm put together.

———

This article originally appeared in the February 2000 issue of *By The Numbers*.

Introduction to "ARM—Average Run Equivalent Method"

Fielding has received much less attention over the years than offense. However, there are still a few different statistics used to evaluate fielders.

Fielding average (FA), of course, is the traditional fielding statistic. But over the last decades researchers have rightly pointed out that FA measures only a fielder's propensity for errors. A fielder's job, however, is not to avoid errors (although that would be a desirable side effect). His job is to turn batted balls into outs. A ground ball bobbled for an E6 is no worse, and perhaps better, than a ground ball that the shortstop never gets to, but the former counts against the fielder where the latter does not.

In the light of that logic, Bill James, in the '70s, invented "Range Factor." This statistic is simply the number of plays per game a fielder makes. It measures what we're interested in – how often a fielder turns balls into outs. And it seems to work reasonably well. Players who have a reputation for defensive excellence, such as Ozzie Smith or Brooks Robinson, routinely have much higher range factors than others.

But Range Factor has its flaws as a player evaluation tool. For one thing, some players are late-inning defensive replacements, and play only one or two innings a game. This artificially lowers their range factor, since each of their "games" is only a fraction of, say, one of Cal Ripken's games. In addition, a player's apparent range would be influenced by whether his team's pitchers struck out a lot of batters (on which no fielder gets a chance to make a play), or whether it was a ground-ball or fly ball staff. Indeed, a player could simply have more balls hit in his direction for no reason other than random luck.

Partly for these reasons, STATS, Inc., came up with "Zone Rating" in the early '90s. STATS simply counted all batted balls hit into the player's area, and counted what portion of these were turned into outs. Computing this statistic does require detailed play-by-play accounts of each game, information which is proprietary to STATS (although available for a price), and information which is available only for recent years. It's impossible, for instance, to retroactively figure out how many balls were hit to Richie Ashburn in 1956. However, Zone Rating is a direct measurement of exactly what we want to know, and, despite these factors, it's considered an excellent tool to evaluate fielders.

Finally, the latest innovation in fielding statistics again comes from Bill James, in his 2002 book, *Win Shares*. James evaluates a player by starting with his raw plays made, but then adjusting for estimated innings played, for team strikeouts, for team defense at other positions (any ball an outfielder misses is another opportunity for the shortstop to make a play next batter), and for the league norm for players at that position. This method requires only traditional statistics readily available throughout baseball history, and can therefore be used for players from any era.

All three of these statistics consider only outs. And, indeed, the player's main job is to turn balls into outs. But if a fielder can't make an out, the outfielder has a secondary job—trying to limit base runner advancement. If Ellis Valentine can't get to that ball hit into the gap, his arm can still keep the runner on first from scoring on the play. He might even throw the runner out, saving his team even more runs.

It is this aspect of outfielder defense that is the subject of this study. Analyzing almost 30 years worth of play-by-play data, Clem Comly figures out how often and how far outfielders let runners advance, and how many runs those players saved or cost their team. To my knowledge, it's the first time this has been done for a large (and therefore statistically significant) number of baseball years.

Which outfielders had the best arms? This is probably the only study that has the evidence to tell you.

Phil Birnbaum

ARM—Average Run Equivalent Method

by Clem Comly

What follows are my findings on a method to analyze more completely the ability of outfielders to shut down the running game. In the past OF assists and anecdotal evidence were used. More recently, the *STATS Baseball Scoreboard* has presented the percentage of runners who have taken the extra base when the opportunity was provided. Let's call this new method ARM (Average Run Equivalent Method). ARM takes into account assists, extra bases taken by either the batter or the runner, and errors made by the outfielder whenever a single is fielded with runners on first and/or second (regardless of the third base runner situation). ARM, which requires play-by-play data, was used for most of the major league games from 1959 to 1987 (thanks to Retrosheet and the Baseball Workshop). Data for different OF positions are kept separate. Among other questions ARM could let us answer is what is the difference between having Greg Luzinski in LF rather than Carl Yastrzemski for a full season (and the answer is not 43 pounds, despite what TB says).

First, we use play-by-play to identify situations where we know a single was hit to a specific outfielder. ARM notes his name, the outs and the runner positions before the hit, and the result. If there was no runner on first or on second, ARM discards the result. If there is also a runner on 3B, 99% of the time we throw that runner away but keep the result of the other runners. The less than 1% of the time where the OF throws out the runner from 3B at home, ARM treats as if the runner on 3B had been on second. Any subsequent infielder error or pickoff of a runner is not recorded as the actual result, but instead a best guess of the result without that extraneous play. The OF gets no credit for the out on the bases unless he gets an assist, but he does get credit for an out when he gets an assist but the runner was actually safe when an infielder dropped the throw for an error.

So in effect there are nine starting states: three out possibilities multiplied by three runner situations: man on first (called "1" below), man on second ("2"), and men on first and second ("12"). For each event from the play-by-play, ARM records the resulting runner positions, any out that was made by the OF's throw (+ below), and any runs scoring (- below for one run scoring). When ARM has finished for a particular OF for a particular position, ARM uses Pete Palmer's expected future runs for the resulting out and base situation and adds 1 for each run scored. Each such expected run result is recorded, and the league average for that OF and that number of outs is subtracted. The sum of all these differences is the ARM total—the number of runs that outfielder saved (or allowed) over the league average. A negative number means the outfielder saved runs (since fewer runs than average scored), and a positive number means that the outfielder cost his team more runs than average.

In the period 1959-1987, for instance, two center fielders with similar raw numbers are shown below:

PLAYER	S	MS	SINGLES W/ 1/2/12	ASSISTS ON SINGLES
Rick Miller	1313	116	539	16
Jose Cardenal	1342	164	561	19

To interpret the headings, in that period the play-by-play showed 1,313 singles hit to CF while Miller was playing there. Some singles in the play-by-play data are anonymous in terms of who fielded them. While Miller was in CF, there were 116 that on a pro rata basis were hit to him which I will call MS (missing singles). (These 116 are strictly to show the level of accuracy of the play-by-play and are not included in the 1,313.) ARM looked at the 539 singles of the 1313 that happened with runners on first and/or second regardless of the runner on 3B. Miller garnered 16 assists after fielding those 539 singles. Looking at Cardenal, both his assist total and his singles fielded are a little higher. Through these traditional stats, the two outfielders' arms look roughly equal.

But the ARMs are significantly different. Calculating the ARM for Miller on those 539 hits gives −9.0, so he saved his team 9 runs for his career from 1959 to 1987 compared to the baseline CF. Cardenal's ARM works out to +5.2, meaning his arm allowed 5.2 more runs to score than the average center fielder's ARM would have allowed.

So even though the two players' traditional numbers look roughly the same, Miller's ARM is much better, by over 14 runs. What happened?

We can find out by first breaking down the three baserunner starting positions which, allowing for rounding, add up to the ARM:

PLAYER	NET RUNS	=NET 1	+NET 2	+NET 12
Rick Miller	-9.0	-2.7	-2.7	-3.5
Jose Cardenal	+5.2	+9.6	-3.6	-0.7

Cardenal's problem, for the most part, is due to his performance with a runner on first without a runner on second. What was the problem? Let's add together the 0 out, 1 out, and 2 out events and compare them to get an idea.

Here's the breakdown, by the situation after the single. (The headings are final baserunner positions—so "13" means runners on first and third—while the "+" means a runner was thrown out, and a "-" means a run scored.)

PLAYER	OPP	1+	2+	3+	12	13	23	1-	2-	3-
					RESULT SITUATIONS					
Rick Miller	292	3	0	1	194	81	4	0	8	1
Jose Cardenal	288	5	1	3	127	126	16	5	4	1

Cardenal threw out more runners (9 (5+1+3) to 4 (3+0+1)) and was only slightly worse in allowing the runner to score from first (10 (5+4+1) to 9 (0+8+1)). Cardenal's problem was the runner was going to third almost half the time (49%, (126+16)/288) while Miller was at 30% ((81+4)/292). ARM balances these factors and shows Miller is more valuable.

Let's look at a Gold Glove versus a hitter, Yaz versus Luzinski:

Yastrzemski

YEAR	GS	S	MS	TS	ARM	A
1961	146	238	16	111	0	6
1962	160	192	89	87	-1	5
1963	150	197	71	74	-2	6
1964	16	30	3	11	-1	1
1965	115	111	100	46	-3	4
1966	151	160	91	63	-8	8
1967	157	194	30	82	-7	8
1968	152	212	44	88	-3	5
1969	138	248	10	108	-7	8
1970	64	126	7	52	-1	0
1971	144	272	9	127	-9	11
1972	82	139	26	71	-1	4
1973	15	36	5	13	1	0
1974	62	82	12	31	0	0
1975	8	4	10	1	0	0
1976	51	113	10	44	-2	2
1977	138	209	57	87	-7	9
1978	63	102	17	47	-1	2
1979	34	56	6	24	-3	1
1980	32	34	6	11	1	0
1983	1	2	0	2	-0	0
TOTAL	1879	2757	630	1010	-56	79

GS	Games Started in LF
S	Singles fielded
MS	Prorated unidentified singles
TS	Singles fielded with a runner on 1B and/or 2B regardless of 3B (excluding MS)
ARM	Equivalent runs minus baseline LF
A	Assists on singles fielded with man on 1B and/or 2B regardless of 3B

Luzinski

YEAR	GS	S	MS	TS	ARM	A
1972	145	145	32	47	2	2
1973	157	199	36	89	-1	5
1974	81	128	3	51	-1	4
1975	159	255	2	111	1	6
1976	144	206	1	71	2	3
1977	148	200	0	86	2	3
1978	154	195	0	70	-3	2
1979	124	185	0	74	3	1
1980	105	148	1	61	2	2
TOTAL	1217	1661	82	660	9	28

Both were starting in LF at age 21 (below are seasons primarily at LF):

												Avg.
Yastrzemski	ARM	0	-1	-2*	-3	-8	-7	-3	-7	-9	-1*	-4.1
Yastrzemski	A	6	5	6	4	8	8	5	8	11	4	6.5

Five years later Yaz will return to LF

											Avg.
Luzinski	ARM	2	-1	-1	1	2	2	-3	3	2	1.3
Luzinski	A	2	5	4	6	3	3	2	1	2	4.0

ARM suggests that Yaz was a better-throwing LF than Luzinski to the tune of over five runs per season.

Now, let's look at the best and worst single-season ARMs for each position:

BEST AND WORST SINGLE SEASON ARMs

LEFT FIELD			CENTER FIELD			RIGHT FIELD		
1978	S.Henderson	-10.7	1976	Beniquez	-12.4	1963	Callison	-10.9
1978	Cromartie	-10.6	1980	O.Moreno	-10.7	1974	G.Gross	-10.6
1985	J.Leonard	-10.5	1983	E.Milner	-10.6	1978	E.Valentin	-10.3
1971	Yastrzemski	-9.5	1978	Dawson	-9.2	1985	Barfield	-10.3
1983	J.Leonard	-8.8	1982	Dw.Murphy	-9.2	1986	vanSlyke	-9.7
1982	Lon.Smith	-8.5	1974	Geronimo	-9.1	1987	Barfield	-8.9
1973	Stargell	-8.3	1972	Unser	-9.0	1977	J.Clark	-8.3
1980	LeFlore	-8.0	1968	Berry	-8.2	1973	K.Singleton	-8.2
1974	Rose	-7.6	1980	Dw.Murphy	-8.2	1986	G.Wilson	-8.0
1966	Yastrzemski	-7.7	1973	Cedeno	-7.7	1987	G.Wilson	-7.7
1971	F.Howard	4.4	1961	K.Hunt	4.0	1984	C.Washington	4.8
1961	Minoso	4.4	1967	Pepitone	4.0	1980	G.Matthews	4.8
1967	J.Alou	4.5	1966	Cleon Jones	4.1	1964	Christopher	4.8
1978	Page	4.7	1968	Reg. Smith	4.3	1975	Burroughs	5.4
1982	Winfield	4.9	1969	Reg. Smith	4.6	1980	Griffey	5.6
1965	F.Howard	5.2	1965	Flood	4.9	1960	J.Cunningham	6.3
1968	F.Howard	5.1	1962	Bruton	5.0	1969	T.Conigliaro	7.1
1975	Kingman	5.1	1968	T.Gonzalez	5.0	1969	K.Harrelson	7.2
1963	L.Wagner	6.0	1970	Cardenal	5.2	1960	Allison	7.3
1964	L.Wagner	6.1	1959	Ashburn	5.8	1977	Burroughs	7.5
1968	R.Allen	6.3	1964	Cowan	5.9	1967	Swoboda	7.8
			1983	G.Thomas	6.9			

And here are the career bests and worsts:

CAREER BEST AND WORST ARMs BY POSITION

LF ARM CAREER 1959-1987				CF ARM CAREER 1959-1987				RF ARM CAREER 1959-1987			
NAME	S	MS	ARM	NAME	S	MS	ARM	NAME	S	MS	ARM
Yaz	2757	630	-56	Dw.Murphy	1461	616	-38	Callison	2189	55	-39
J. Rice	2006	958	-26	Cedeno	2165	632	-35	Barfield	854	437	-38
Wil.Wilson	1103	48	-24	Geronimo	1557	133	-29	Clemente	2257	478	-34
Stargell	1507	314	-21	Dawson	1652	272	-29	J.Clark	1324	148	-28
J.Leonard	643	490	-21	G.Maddox	2609	375	-28	E.Valentine	1058	174	-26
Lon.Smith	740	418	-20	Blair	2472	343	-27	Dw.Evans	2163	912	-25
Raines	891	346	-19	O.Moreno	1966	240	-26	O.Brown	1030	148	-23
R.Henderson	1050	270	-18	W. Mays	3206	618	-26	Glen.Wilson	606	368	-20
Cromartie	649	142	-17	Dal.Murphy	1207	703	-25	Hank Aaron	1775	352	-18
George Bell	472	365	-15	Willi.Davis	3740	201	-24	Parker	2157	511	-18
Oglivie	1783	468	-15	Unser	1995	94	-23	Winfield	1784	611	-17
Page	386	119	7	Mota	306	54	5	Al Cowens	1627	483	-17
H.Lopez	686	36	8	K.Gibson	234	48	5	G. Gross	497	141	-16
Hinton	628	39	8	Hisle	911	90	5	M.Hershberger	647	296	-16
Brock	3366	308	8	Cardenal	1342	164	5	Pinson	648	60	11
Luzinski	1661	82	9	J.Briggs	476	13	5	K.Harrelson	333	32	11
Al.Johnson	1448	64	9	Cowan	363	19	6	Singleton	1571	285	12
R.White	2613	181	10	Landis	1556	292	6	J.Cunningham	401	11	12
Baylor	994	111	10	Pepitone	579	10	7	Murcer	1161	78	13
Covington	710	60	12	Lenny Green	922	115	7	Fr.Robinson	1355	226	15
L.Wagner	1228	273	21	T.Gonzalez	1503	78	8	C.Washington	1164	435	15
F.Howard	1290	19	22	Ashburn	608	39	12	Allison	822	20	16
								Burroughs	1108	83	20

Conclusions

The key point of this study is we now have an idea of how much outfield throwing talent can be worth. The difference from absolute best season to worst is about two victories (around 20 runs). This is a combination of:

- the limited number of opportunities in a season (usually 50-100 singles with a runner on 1B and/or 2B),
- the talent is one of degree not kind, and
- the refusal of managers to keep putting a real rag arm in the field.

From season to season, even the best don't average saving their teams even one victory compared to an average OF. Of course, the average RF in 1964 was 10% Callison and 10% Clemente. Speaking of Clemente, a Pirate pitcher was quoted on SABR-L as saying that Clemente liked to show off his arm by throwing to third base where there wasn't a play, allowing the batter to get to second and thus hurting the Pirates. Clemente's ARM reflects batters taking second, so overall he didn't hurt the Pirates (as his Gold Gloves also attest to).

As Retrosheet holdings expand toward the present and further into the past, ARM can be calculated for more outfielders in baseball history. This methodology can be used for other studies; the one that most immediately springs to mind is baserunner evaluation. Obviously, the average result of a single to LF with a runner on 1B is the result for the average left fielder is in large part the result of the average runner on 1B.

Disclaimers

I purposely chose singles only because extra-base hits are much more a function of the ballpark. Also, the sample size is low for singles, for doubles and triples. ARM is limited to the accuracy of the play-by-play data files, which no CPA would sign. More than 95%, but not 100%, of the games were available for the period 1959-1987. There may also be a slight bias that anonymous singles will tend to be hits on which no assist or error occurred. The baseline RF, CF, and LF were the averages of three ML seasons, 1961, 1966, 1968, and the NL of 1962 and 1969 (which were chosen because of availability at the beginning of the project). For most seasons, the sum of all outfielders is a little better than zero. I call this "ARM", but it also measures the judgment of the OF and his ability to get into position to throw. Obviously, there may have been some singles that Yaz left his feet on that Luzinski let get by him for extra bases. ARM punishes Yaz for letting the runner go to third on those singles. Defensive average or range factor, which ARM supplements and does not replace, should reward Yaz for that play.

This article originally appeared in the August 2000 issue of *By The Numbers*.

Introduction to
"Do Faster Runners Induce More Fielding Errors?"

At first glance, it might seem that sabermetrics underrates the value of speed. Many of the basic offensive statistics, like Runs Created and On-base Plus Slugging, don't consider a player's stolen bases. Those that do, assign them a fairly small value. Further, research has shown that stolen bases don't help a team all that much—a successful stolen base is worth only a fifth of a run, less than half the value of a single. And players who are caught stealing more than a third of the time are costing their teams runs, no matter how large the number in their SB column.

But despite appearances, offensive statistics do, in fact, take speed into account. When Rickey Henderson beats out an infield single, it shows up in his batting line as a base hit, whereas a slower player would easily have been out on the same play. When Mo Vaughn hits a sure double into the gap, but the outfielder quickly chases it down and holds the slow-footed DH to first base, Mo gets credit for only a single.

Faster players tend to ground into fewer double plays. Jorge Posada led the American League in 2002 in GIDP with 23. Had he hit a more reasonable 12, say, he would have saved his team about half a win. Again, that shows up in the batting line. The full version of Runs Created includes an adjustment for GIDP, and Posada's lack of speed would be taken into account there.

Then, there's the fielder's choice effect. When the batter hits a grounder with a fast runner on first base, the runner's speed forces the defense to go for the play at first. That means that instead of (say) two outs and a runner on first, there are two outs and a runner on second. This certainly has value, perhaps a fifth of a run per occurrence, but doesn't happen often enough to be a large component of a player's value. Still, this is one positive contribution of speed that does not show up in the batting line.

But offsetting this, there is a way in which the batting line "overrates" a batter's speed. In general, for a hit, a slow player needs to hit the ball harder than a fast player. A Luis Castillo double could be a lightly hit ball that Luis ran hard on. But a Cecil Fielder double has to be a booming shot in the gap to the wall if Cecil is going to reach second base. And so, faster players' doubles will see fewer runners advancing, and their batting line will overestimate their ability to advance runners.

The bottom line, then, so far is a wash. Most of a runner's speed is reflected in the batting line, and one factor that's not, the fielder's choice effect, is to some extent cancelled by the advancement effect.

We are left with at least one other factor we haven't yet considered—reaching base on errors. When the third baseman bobbles a grounder, he may still have time to throw out the fat guy, but not the fast guy. Speedy runners will then reach base more often than average, but since reaching on an error doesn't show up in the batting line, they may not get credit.

Here, Dan Levitt and Clifford Blau, in separate studies, address this issue. Is the ability to reach base on errors one that forms a significant part of a fast player's value? If so, we should keep in mind that fast players are shortchanged by the traditional sabermetric batting statistics. But if not, the value of a fast batter is already reflected in his batting line.

PHIL BIRNBAUM

Do Faster Runners Induce More Fielding Errors? Two Studies

1. SPEED AND OPPOSITION ERRORS

by Dan Levitt

In the 1997 Statistical Analysis Committee meeting, some of the discussion revolved around the effect of speed as a factor in forcing opposition errors. I have completed some preliminary research in this area, although analyzed for teams rather than individuals.

My study compares team speed scores with opposition errors and opposition unearned runs to check if any correlation exists between team speed and forcing errors. Bill James' Speed Score is used as a proxy for team speed; the calculation is outlined below. Data for opposition errors and unearned runs is from *The Sporting News*.

For comparison purposes I also checked the correlation with the Runs–Runs Created differential. The theory being that a fast team might be more likely to outperform its runs created projection by causing additional errors, taking the extra base or other things that runs created does not count.

The analysis uses 1996 and 1997 data; I have not found available data for opposition errors from earlier publicly available sources. The Runs - Runs Created calculation could obviously be further looked at by using previous years.

The results can be seen below:

Correlation of Speed score with:	Opposition Errors	.42
	Unearned Runs	.26
	(R minus RC)%	.27

Based on taking statistic courses many years ago as an engineering major, I would suggest that the data indicates a positive but not overwhelming relationship between team speed and opposition errors.

Specifically, the top five fastest teams averaged 134 opposition errors, the top ten 127. The slowest five teams averaged 109, and the slowest ten teams 113 opposition errors.

Clearly, only two years of data may not be enough to fully clarify the relationships between speed and opposition errors. Additionally, speed scores may not be the ideal proxy for team speed. For example, it may cause more opposition errors to have several very fast players and several very slow players than a team of all players with average speed—both of which may have similar team speed scores.

The top ten speed scores from 1996 and 1997:

Team	Year	SPS	OE	UR	(R-RC)%
Colorado	1996	6.42	140	72	0.011
Pittsburgh	1997	6.36	137	78	-0.040
Kansas City	1996	6.08	133	75	-0.007
Houston	1996	6.02	121	90	-0.006
Houston	1997	5.94	137	85	-0.023
Minnesota	1997	5.92	100	61	-0.009
Cincinnati	1997	5.88	120	74	-0.077
Pittsburgh	1996	5.86	135	81	0.006
Minnesota	1996	5.82	125	86	0.017
Cincinnati	1996	5.80	123	69	-0.002

The bottom ten speed scores from 1996 and 1997:

Team	Year	SPS	OE	UR	(R-RC)%
California	1996	4.06	112	58	-0.070
Boston	1997	4.37	110	66	-0.085
Oakland	1996	4.54	95	49	-0.022
Oakland	1997	4.62	93	55	-0.063
Atlanta	1996	4.72	135	75	-0.033
Detroit	1996	4.78	103	62	0.048
Florida	1996	4.81	115	54	-0.036
New York	1997	4.87	116	83	0.045
Atlanta	1997	4.89	132	83	-0.023
Cleveland	1997	4.91	120	67	-0.064

Where:

SPS - Speed Score, as described in the 1988 Bill James *Baseball Abstract*, but excluding the range factor component.
OE - Opponents errors.
UR - Unearned runs scored.
(R − RC)% - Actual runs less runs created as a percentage of runs.

———

This article originally appeared in the October 1998 issue of *By The Numbers*.

2. REACHING BASE ON ERRORS

by Cliff Blau

A previous study by Tom Ruane looked at the relative costs of strikeouts, groundouts, and fly outs. In part because he included times that batters reached base on errors (and unsuccessful fielder's choices) in outs, he found that groundouts were the least costly. I thought that this information could be useful in creating run-scoring models.

Subsequently, Tom supplied some data on how many times each hitter had reached base on error (henceforth ROE) from 1980 to 1998. I compared these data to other statistics to see if a model could be developed that would predict a hitter's ROE average.

I initially performed a multivariate regression analysis using the following factors, each on a per-at-bat basis: hits, doubles, triples, home runs, strikeouts, sacrifice flies, stolen bases, and grounded into double plays. I also used the hitter's batting side. Despite finding a strong relationship using a limited data set, once I tried the analysis with the full sample, I found almost no correlation between those factors and ROE. After eliminating all players with fewer than 1,000 at-bats, the correlation was .264.

I next divided players up into groups with certain characteristics. One such group consisted of right-handed hitters who ground into double plays a lot, while another was left-handed hitters who rarely ground into double plays. I also compared right-handed and left-handed home run hitters who strike out frequently. While the average player in the sample ROE'd 14 times per 1,000 at bats, the group expected to reach most often, right-handed ground ball hitters, had an average ROE of 15.5 times per 1,000 at bats, while the upper-cutting left-handers ROE'd 10.4 times per 1000 at bats. Using other groups, I found the difference between right-handed and left-handed hitters to be about 3 or 4 ROE per 1,000 at bats. For every extra 100 strikeouts, a batter could be expected to ROE 1.5 fewer times. Speed also had a slight relationship; those stealing bases at three times the average rate had an ROE average .001 higher than normal. A similarly small, opposite relationship exists for slow runners. No relationship was apparent between grounding into double plays and ROE.

Some other authors have looked at this question. Bill James studied how often Texas Ranger players reached base on error in the 1983 season. He concluded that right-handed batters ROE almost 30% more often than lefties, and fast runners ROE 12% more often than slow runners. In his 1986 *Abstract* he reported that on the 1985 Mariners, right-handed hitters reached base just slightly more often than lefties, but fast runners made it 16% more often than slow runners. Mark Pankin, in his article "Subtle Aspects of the Game," used Project Scoresheet data for all major league games from 1984 to 1992. He found that fast runners and right-handed hitters reach base on errors more often. The advantage for righties overwhelmed the speed factor; slow right-handed batters reach base on errors more than fast lefties do.

In summary, just as evaluating fielders by fielding average is not very meaningful because the differences are so small, the same holds true for hitters. If one is rating a hitter who seems to be at one extreme or the other in ROE, one should keep in mind that the hitter is a little more or less valuable than popular formulas such as Runs Created or Linear Weights would suggest.

This article originally appeared in the May 1999 issue of *By The Numbers*.

Introduction to "Clutch Hitting One More Time"

Does clutch hitting exist? This question has been one of the most researched and most debated questions in baseball analysis. Before we go any further, though, it's important that we understand what the question is really asking.

In the most obvious sense, of course clutch hitting exists. When Francisco Cabrera hit that single in the 1992 NLCS, could that have been anything other than a clutch hit? And baseball's greatest home runs—Bobby Thomson, Bill Mazeroski, Bucky Dent, Carlton Fisk — those all exist, and those all were clutch.

Then, of course, there are players who have hit well in certain situations over a longer period of time. Reggie Jackson is "Mr. October." Pat Tabler's bases-loaded record (.579, .556, and .857 in 1983, 1984, and 1985, respectively) is legendary. And Barry Bonds' poor postseason record (before 2002, anyway), was certainly unexpected. These are not in dispute. The question "Have some players hit well or poorly in the clutch over an extended period of time?" is *not* the question we are discussing here.

What the clutch hitting question is really asking is this: Are there some players who *intrinsically* hit better (or worse) in certain "clutch" situations than at other times? Is clutch hitting a *skill*, like hitting for a high average, that players possess to a greater or lesser degree? There are two possibilities:

1. Yes, clutch hitting is a skill that some players have to varying degrees, and previous clutch performance is indicative of future clutch performance; or
2. No, players who hit better or worse in the clutch have simply been lucky or unlucky, and are likely to return to normal clutch hitting in future.

The evidence so far overwhelmingly supports the second hypothesis—that clutch performance is not a skill that any player has. Since the conclusion is so different from fans' and journalists' instincts and intuitions, it's important to be able to understand the reasoning that leads to that conclusion. There are at least a couple of ways you can examine the evidence.

The first is to take last year's best clutch hitters and see how they do this year. If clutch hitting is a skill, you would expect that players who hit well in the clutch last year would do so again this year, just as last year's RBI leaders are more likely to be on this year's RBI list. But if clutch hitting is not a skill, last year's great clutch hitters would be this year's average clutch hitters.

This approach was taken by the *Elias Baseball Analyst* in 1985, in their essay, "Clutch Hitters: They *Do* Exist." Their conclusion, hotly disputed by Bill James (and Rob Neyer), is that the best clutch hitters were still better than average the next year (although to a lesser extent), and that this was evidence of clutch skill.

The second approach is to look at a large group of players and list how all of them performed in the clutch. You then compare those records to how these players would be expected to perform if clutch hitting was just luck. If they're roughly the same, that supports the theory that clutch hitting is random. But if the actual players have widely differing clutch records from the "just luck" case, that's evidence that clutch hitting exists.

This study, by Pete Palmer, takes the second approach. It is perhaps the most comprehensive of studies on this issue, and the conclusion is based on a very strong foundation of data.

PHIL BIRNBAUM

Clutch Hitting One More Time

by Pete Palmer

When the *Elias Baseball Analyst* published at-bat figures for their leaders in various game situations, it allowed for an analysis of the variance between normal and special situations. There is a handy formula which allows you to find what kind of difference would be expected by chance and whether the actual differences found are greater than what would be anticipated. The formula assumes that batting is a binomial distribution where each event has a constant probability of success or failure. The probability of success (P) is simply the batting average, while the probability of failure (Q) is simply (1-BA). The only other number needed is the number of at-bats (N). The formula is

$$\sigma = [(P \times Q)/N]^{.5}$$

For example, for a BA = .250, with 600 at-bats, $\sigma = [(.25 \times .75)/(600)]^{.5} = 0.018$.

The binomial theorem tells us that, with a sufficiently large sample, about 2/3 of the values in the distribution will fall within one standard deviation (σ) of the mean, and that about 95% of the values will fall within 2σ of the mean. In the example, 2/3 of the values in the distribution would be BAs between .232 and .268, while 95% of the BAs would fall between .214 and .286.

When comparing samples (x and y) of two different sizes, the formula used is the formula for a pooled standard deviation, or $\sigma_{xy} = [(P_x Q_x/N_x) + (P_y Q_y/N_y)]^{.5}$

For example, if a player has 236 hits in 671 at-bats in late-inning pressure situations (a .352 BA) while going 1,083 for 3,660 (.296) otherwise, we can calculate a pooled standard deviation as

$$\sigma_{xy} = [(.352 \times .648/671) + (.296 \times .704/3660)]^{.5}$$
$$= [.000340 + .000057]^{.5}$$
$$= [.000397]^{.5} = 0.020$$

The next step is to figure out the expected difference (BA_x - BA_y) between the two situations. This is something which is often left out by analysts, who assume that the expected difference is zero. Because pitchers bear down more in the clutch and because ace relief pitchers are more apt to be used in late-inning pressure situations, the overall batting average is about 10 points lower in these situations. League figures as shown in the *Elias Analyst* indicate only a six-point drop in BA, but the error in this number is about two points. Also we do not have league data for the full 10-year period covered by the data presented. Using a difference of 10 points balances the number of extremes between the high and the low figures. If we used a drop-off in BA of six points, the number of extreme cases would be the same, but more of them would be negative rather than positive differences. If you assumed that there is no drop-off in clutch situations, then you would conclude that the number of hitters with higher BAs in clutch situations is smaller than that expected by chance.

The data I used in the example of calculating a pooled standard deviation is for Tim Raines, the leading late-inning pressure hitter. His difference is (.352- .296), or +56 points in "clutch" situations. The expected difference is -10 points, so his overall difference is +66. If you divide this by the 20-point σ (calculated on the basis of Raines' performance data), you get a z-score of 3.3. Raines' BA in late-inning pressure situations is 3.3 standard deviations higher than his BA in other situations. Now a z-score of 2.0 should occur, *by chance*, about 5% of the time, half on the positive side of the distribution and half on the negative side. We can rephrase this by saying that about 2.5% of all hitters should have clutch BAs which are two standard deviations (or more) above their BAs in other situations, while about 2.5% of all hitters should have clutch BAs which are two standard deviations (or more) below their BAs in other situations. A z-score of ± 3.0 or more should occur only about once in 800 observations.

The lifetime data in the *Analyst* covers all players in the past 10 years with at least 250 at-bats in late-inning pressure situations (or at least about 1,500 at-bats overall for the average player in this group). There have been about 330 such players in the past 10 years, so one would expect about one player to have a z-score of 3 or more (in either the positive or negative direction). There was, in fact, one such player—Tim Raines.

We would expect about 16 players to have z-scores in excess of 2.0 (about 8 positives and 8 negatives); there were 14. Looking at the 1988 leaders, there were 10 players (out of 210 listed; 50 or more "clutch" at-bats or about 300 total at-bats) with z-scores of +2.0 or greater (5% of the total), just as expected. (The highs and lows for the 10-year data run are listed in Table 1.) In short, over the past 10 years, and in 1988, the distribution of performances in late-inning pressure situations appears to conform to a random binomial distribution. It does not provide evidence for the presence of clutch ability.

TABLE 1.
10-YEAR CLUTCH BATTING AVERAGE AND DEVIATIONS FROM EXPECTED BATTING AVERAGES

	AMERICAN LEAGUE				NATIONAL LEAGUE		
PLAYER	CLUTCH BA	OTHER BA	Z	PLAYER	CLUTCH BA	OTHER BA	Z
Raines	.352	.296	3.30	G.Davis	.228	.269	-1.24
Sax	.318	.277	2.54	Scioscia	.228	.269	-1.36
G.Iorg	.306	.252	2.42	Webster	.237	.283	-1.40
R.Henderson	.319	.288	2.17	Bonnell	.235	.279	-1.46
Newman	.269	.214	2.15	Grubb	.225	.276	-1.47
Fernandez	.336	.293	2.07	Doran	.236	.278	-1.56
Manning	.277	.244	2.01	G.Brock	.204	.251	-1.57
Hoffman	.287	.237	2.01	Foli	.220	.269	-1.62
Cester	.290	.261	1.94	Benedict	.205	.252	-1.66
B.Diaz	.285	.253	1.90	L.Smith	.248	.295	-1.68
Milbourne	.304	.259	1.84	Butler	.242	.287	-1.68
Bosley	.310	.261	1.83	Morrison	.227	.270	-1.69
C.Brown	.309	.264	1.77	Bittner	.227	.293	-1.76
Coleman	.291	.258	1.66	J.Davis	.213	.259	-1.83
R.Roenicke	.269	.228	1.65	Randolph	.235	.281	-1.95
L.Salazar	.286	.260	1.61	Kittle	.186	.245	-1.95
C.Moore	.289	.263	1.55	Heath	.211	.259	-1.97
Tolleson	.272	.245	1.43	Lynn	.237	.285	-2.06
Wiggins	.284	.255	1.42	Gladden	.220	.281	-2.12
Foley	.283	.255	1.30	Burleson	.215	.282	-2.28
Staub	.295	.267	1.29	S.Owen	.184	.250	-2.41
Yeager	.238	.212	1.25	Heep	.194	.265	-2.43
B.Wills	.289	.262	1.24	Rice	.245	.305	-2.88

This article originally appeared in the March 1990 issue of *By The Numbers*.

Introduction to "Does Good Hitting Beat Good Pitching?"

In this article Tom Hanrahan picks a fight with one of the trickiest of baseball aphorisms and wrestles it to a draw. As Hanrahan illustrates so effectively, the problem with baseball's wisdom many times is not so much knowing whether the adage is true, but knowing what it means. Baseball's talmudic wisdom is often stated in opaque generalizations, the unraveling of which is akin to trying to beat a straight answer out of the Delphic oracle. Like a police officer charging a suspect with everything from loitering to menacing, in the hope of finding something that will stick, Hanrahan states the practical import of the generalization in each of the specific terms that *might* be covered by it, and finds them all wanting (or not—don't want to give away the surprise ending). It is not true that this convinces no one; it convinces me. We have long since given up on convincing Connie Mack or, for that matter, anyone given to *quoting* Connie Mack. Studying the evidence is the best we can do; forcing others to believe it is beyond the ambitions of sane people.

BILL JAMES

Does Good Hitting Beat Good Pitching?

by Tom Hanrahan

A Bit of Background

"Good pitching will beat good hitting." This adage is much older than I, and so it is with much humility and respect that I attempt to debunk it, yet while affirming it to be true in some senses.

First, when we ask this question, we need to define what we mean. Does the phrase "good pitching will beat good hitting" mean when two good teams collide, the team with the better pitching will win more often?

- If Pedro is on the mound and he has his good stuff, it doesn't really matter who is batting?
- The run-generating abilities of Vlad Guerrero or Todd Helton impact the outcome of an at-bat less than the run-preventing abilities of an ace pitcher?
- All of the above?
- Something else?

The question could be answered differently, depending on what is meant.

Also, when looking for evidence to answer this question, we need to take care not to confuse causal factors with coincidental ones. For example:

Fact: *There are fewer runs scored in your typical post-season game than in the regular season.* Is this evidence for the old adage? Or is it proof that fewer runs are scored when you don't need a fifth starting pitcher and when it's colder outside?

Fact: *Teams which allow 150 fewer runs than the league average will win more games and pennants than teams which score 150 more runs than the league average.* Does this prove pitching's superiority? Or does it imply that it's easier to build a winning team in a pitcher's park, or show that by allowing fewer runs your ratio of runs scored to runs allowed is better than by scoring extra runs?

The Question Defined

Here is how I will *not* define the question: *Is a run saved more valuable than a run gained?*

The answer to this question, I believe, is yes, but it isn't relevant to our topic. Many studies have shown that a team's ratio of run scored to runs allowed correlates very well with a team's wins. It is very easy to see that if the league average for a team is 800 runs per year, lowering your runs allowed by 100 (down to 700) makes your ratio 1.143. In order to achieve a team ratio of 1.143 by scoring additional runs, the team runs scored would have to be $800 \times 1.143 = 914$. This means 100 runs saved has the same value in this example as 114 runs scored, so these runs saved are 14% more important. This has relevant applications to simulation games, MVP awards, and debates of Roger Clemens' value versus Barry Bonds', but it has no real bearing on what happens when Clemens faces Bonds.

Here is how I *will* define the question: *When superior batters face superior pitchers, are the results different from expectations predicted by using typical mathematical models of their abilities?*

In other words, Mark McGwire hits lots of home runs (when he's healthy). Greg Maddux does not allow many home runs. If McGwire hits three times as many dingers as the typical batter, but Maddux only allows one-third as a typical pitcher, what happens when they face each other? The expectation would be that given these inputs, McGwire would hit an approximately average amount of home runs in his at-bats against Maddux. If in reality McGwire hits *fewer* home runs in his appearances against Maddux, then we can say that in this instance, good pitching has indeed stopped good hitting.

Specific Methods

I approached the question two ways. The first was a study based solely on batting average. I chose this as my first metric because the data were available, because of its common use, and because Dan Levitt had used this method in the February 1999 *By the Numbers* ("The Batter/Pitcher Matchup," pp. 18-20), so I would have a point of comparison. The second study was an attempt to look at the whole picture of run scoring and prevention, since there could be effects other than batting average. For this second study I found records of individual matchups of batter versus pitcher, and was able to compare expected to actual on base and slugging averages.

The paper by Dan Levitt quoted a formula used by Bill James in his 1983 *Baseball Abstract* which yields the expected batting average, given the hitter batting average, the pitcher batting average allowed, and the league batting average. Once again this is reproduced here:

Expected batting average =

$$\frac{(\text{BAT AVG}) \times (\text{PIT AVG})/(\text{LG AVG})}{(\text{BAT AVG}) \times (\text{PIT AVG})/(\text{LG AVG}) + (1 - \text{BAT AVG}) \times (1 - \text{PIT AVG})/(1 - \text{LG AVG})}$$

He used a sample of all hitters with at least 446 plate appearances and all pitchers with at least 100 batters faced in the 1995 season, and found the formula accurately predicted reality.

The database I used here is from the years 1984-1996. There is a total of almost 1.4 million at-bats when both leagues are combined. The database recorded all batters who hit for a certain average during a specific year, and how they fared when batting against pitchers who allowed a certain batting average in that year. The averages are divided into "bins" every .005 points.

Copying Dan's approach, I divided all hitters and pitchers into three groups (good, average, and poor) according to batting average by combining the "bins." This yielded a block of nine comparisons for each league (good vs. good, good vs. average, etc.). For each block I computed the batting average expected by the formula to that actually achieved. The results? The formula predicted the actual totals very, very accurately.

Table 1 gives the data for the American League, Table 2 the National. Here is how to calculate the formula-predicted batting average: find the opponents' average for good pitchers in the right-most column of all batters in Table 1 (.2374). Then find the average for good hitters in the bottom row of all pitchers (.3006). An extra decimal place is used to reduce rounding errors. The overall league average (bottom row, right) is .2652.

Table 1. AMERICAN LEAGUE

PLAYER CATEGORY	POOR BATTERS (BA < .253)	AVERAGE BATTERS (.252<BA<.283)	GOOD BATTERS (BA > .282)	ALL BATTERS
GOOD PITCHERS (OPP AVG < .253)				
AT-BATS	93137	106936	81393	281466
HITS	19215	25320	22272	66807
BATTING AVG	.2063	.2368	.2736	.2374
AVERAGE PITCHERS (.252 < AVG < .283)				
AT-BATS	93321	111247	86180	290748
HITS	21995	29988	26020	78003
BATTING AVG	.2357	.2696	.3019	.2683
POOR PITCHERS (OPP AVG > .282)				
AT-BATS	63793	77928	61820	203541
HITS	16822	23437	20664	60923
BATTING AVG	.2637	.3080	.3343	.2993
ALL PITCHERS				
AT-BATS	250251	296111	229393	775755
HITS	58032	78745	68956	205733
BATTING AVG	.2319	.2659	.3006	.2652

Table 2. NATIONAL LEAGUE

PLAYER CATEGORY	POOR BATTERS (BA < .253)	AVERAGE BATTERS (.252<BA<.283)	GOOD BATTERS (BA > .282)	ALL BATTERS
GOOD PITCHERS (OPP AVG < .253)				
AT-BATS	63914	80218	55085	199217
HITS	13011	19084	14810	46905
BATTING AVG	.2036	.2379	.2689	.2354
AVERAGE PITCHERS (.252 < AVG < .283)				
AT-BATS	57020	74962	55227	187209
HITS	13121	19744	16503	49368
BATTING AVG	.2301	.2634	.2988	.2637
POOR PITCHERS (OPP AVG > .282)				
AT-BATS	64197	89963	67403	221563
HITS	16878	26386	21905	65169
BATTING AVG	.2629	.2933	.3250	.2941
ALL PITCHERS				
AT-BATS	185131	245143	177715	607989
HITS	43010	62514	53218	161442
BATTING AVG	.2323	.2660	.2995	.2655

Using the formula, the predicted batting average resulting from these circumstances is (.2374 × .3006/.2652) / [(.2374 × .3006/.2652) + (.7626 × .6994/.7348)] = .2704. The actual average achieved was .2736. The good batters actually hit 3 points better than expected against the good pitchers, over the course of over 81,000 at-bats.

Table 3. ACTUAL RESULTS COMPARED TO EXPECTED BATTING AVERAGE DIFFERENCES

PLAYER CATEGORY	LEAGUE	POOR BATTERS	AVERAGE BATTERS	GOOD BATTERS
GOOD PITCHERS	AL	0	-1	3
AVERAGE PITCHERS	AL	1	1	-2
POOR PITCHERS	AL	0	1	-3
GOOD PITCHERS	NL	-1	2	2
AVERAGE PITCHERS	NL	-1	-1	1
POOR PITCHERS	NL	4	-1	-5
GOOD PITCHERS	MLB	-1	0	3
AVERAGE PITCHERS	MLB	0	0	0
POOR PITCHERS	MLB	2	0	-4

Table 3 gives a summary of how each batter versus pitcher combination fared as compared to the formula prediction, when the data from both leagues is combined. Every category was within 5 points of batting average of the predictions. For the sample sizes used, up to 3 or 4 points difference could be explained by random chance. The only difference that is statistically significant is for the case of good batters facing poor pitchers. The standard deviation of the batting average, as calculated using the binomial method, for both leagues combined would be .0013 ([.3294 × (1-.3294)/129223]^0.5). The hitters batted 4 points lower, which is 3 standard deviations lower. However, even though this is statistically significant, it is not practically significant—a MLB manager may have a difficult time finding a way to take advantage of the knowledge that good hitters pound lousy pitchers by a whole 4 points less than expected.

So what does this mean? I conclude that in terms of batting average, good pitching does *not* beat good hitting. Batters hit pretty much what was expected, given the quality of pitching they faced. If anything, there is a hint of evidence that the good hitters may fare a bit better than expected against good pitchers.

A Different Approach

I mentioned previously a second method of study, based on on-base and slugging averages. This was undertaken since it is certainly possible that the ability to produce or prevent runs would show up in the batter/pitcher matchup in ways that are not represented by batting average alone. STATS, Inc. produces an annual book entitled *Match-Ups!* The 1997 version gives individual batter vs. pitcher data for all players active at the end of the 1996 season.

Following the same approach as in the other study, I divided both hitters and pitchers into groups labeled good, poor, and average. I found all hitters active as of September 1996 who had more than 3,000 career at-bats, and pitchers with greater than 800 innings pitched. The hitters were grouped by Runs Created per Game (the formula used in the *Bill James Historical Abstract*, first edition), and the pitchers by ERA. There were 110 hitters and 85 pitchers in the study, of which 36 hitters and 27 pitchers were each classified as "good." Their totals, both composite and for pitchers divided by group, are given in Table 4 (the other pitchers' totals are shown only for comparison). They are not used in the study, as I only was interested in the matchup of good hitters against good pitchers; besides, it would have been nine times as much work to record and calculate all of the other combinations. It should be noted that the ERA of the pitchers in the study is better than the overall league average. Obviously, pitchers and hitters who had a large amount of playing time are typically better than "average," so the labels given to the groups might be misnomers in a sense. This study may actually be using some of the top quarter or fifth of all pitchers and hitters in this period, but that does not affect the methods used or the conclusions.

Table 4. BATTER VS. PITCHER MATCHUP DATA CAREER RECORDS, 1984-1996

PLAYER CATEGORY	IP	WEIGHTED ERA
GOOD PITCHERS (ERA < 3.53)	43116	3.28
AVERAGE PITCHERS (3.53 < ERA <3.90)	41105	3.74
POOR PITCHERS (ERA > 3.90)	42105	4.16
ALL PITCHERS WITH > 800 IP	126326	3.72

PLAYER CATEGORY	AB	R/G	OPS
GOOD HITTERS (R/G > 5.9)	178654	6.28	.860

The main difference between this method and the first is that the groupings are based on career statistics, not individual seasons. Reasonable arguments can be made about the advantages of either method.

Data for pitchers' SLG allowed was not available. However, this can be derived from the opponents' OBA and ERA. The league averages for the period 1984-1996, weighted by player-years active in study, were OBA = .3274, SLG = .3988, and ERA = 4.074. From this we can relate ERA to the offensive components by the formula ERA = OBA × SLG × 31.20 for this period, using the accepted structure for Runs Created. Since this formula works for leagues (the RMS error in computing ERA for individual seasons using the formula was 0.08, or 2% of the ERA), I have assumed it works for individual pitchers.

For the good pitchers, their OBA allowed = .3009. SLG is defined as = ERA / OBA / 31.2 = 3.283 / .3009 / 31.2 = .3497. We infer this as the slugging percentage allowed by the good pitchers.

GOOD PITCHERS OBA = .3009, SLG = .3497
GOOD HITTERS OBA = .3790, SLG = .4807
LEAGUE AVG OBA = .3274, SLG =.3988

Formula predicted results of good pitchers vs. good hitters:

OBA = (.3009 × .3790/.3274) / (.3009 × .3788/.3274 + .6991 × .6210/.6726) = .3505

SLG = (.3497 × .4807/.3988) / (.3497 × .4807/.3988 + .6503 × .5193/.6012) = .4287

What were the actual results? Drumroll, please.

   In 16,564 at-bats of good hitters versus good pitchers: OBA = .3501, SLG = .4545

Table 5.
GOOD HITTERS RECORDS VS. GOOD PITCHERS DEFINED BY CAREER DATA, 1984-1996

	ACTUAL	PREDICTED	DIFFERENCE
OBA	.3501	.3505	-.0004
SLG	.4545	.4287	+.0258

Table 5 shows that when facing good pitchers good hitters had an OBA almost exactly as expected by the formula prediction. The SLG, however, was 26 points higher! Is this a significant difference statistically? Calculating a standard deviation of SLG is not as simple as batting average, since there are multiple event possibilities, but by Monte Carlo simulation I came up with a σ(SLG) for 16,564 at bats = .0058. This means that a difference of 26 points is *definitely* statistically significant (over four standard deviations!). The larger chance for error here is not mathematical, but rather is in my assumption of how to infer slugging average allowed for pitchers. However, it seems unlikely to me that the formula would be off by as much as the 6% difference between expected SLG and actual SLG, since the error for predicting league ERAs for each year was only 2%.

Conclusions

Does good pitching stop good hitting? No more so than anyone should expect. A pitcher who allows few hits and walks will surrender proportionately fewer of these regardless of the class of hitter at the plate. Manny Ramirez is likely to garner more hits against poor pitchers, but he will still hit his share against good ones.
   There is some evidence to suggest that it is possible, although I'm not sure I should say "likely," that in terms of power, good hitting might actually beat good pitching. I recommend a study that focuses on home runs, using a larger sample than my second study here, to see if this is true.

This article originally appeared in the August 2001 issue of *By The Numbers*.

Introduction to "Offensive Replacement Levels"

There's an established Bill James creation called the "defensive spectrum." It's just a specific ordering of the fielding positions:

DH   1B   LF   RF   3B   CF   2B   SS

The idea behind the spectrum is that the positions to the right of the spectrum are more difficult to play than those on the left. All things being equal, players who play (for instance) second base are more valuable than those who play left field.

To accept this hypothesis, we need to test it. And so, we can ask, if this were true, what would the implications be? One important implication is that players on the left end of the spectrum should be more likely to lose their jobs, for a given level of offense, than players on the right. For instance, a right fielder who hits .250 with no power should be more likely to be released than a shortstop who hits .250 with no power.

And they do, as the data in Cliff Blau's study will confirm.

*   *   *   *

There's another very interesting hypothesis from Bill James. He once suggested that there should be a certain skill level, for each position, where the rate of players getting released changes dramatically. Play this well, and you keep your job, but drop a fraction below that, and you're gone.

To get a better feel for what that means, imagine that your local store is selling a packet of dollar bills for $20. If the packets contain 50 bills, you'll find customers out the door and three miles down the street. If it's 30 one-dollar bills for twenty bucks, the lineup might go down to a mile and a half. At 21 bills per pack, there will still be a line-up, and even at 20 bills plus a dime, there will still be takers. But if the packs contain only 19 bills and ninety cents, the store will be empty. Twenty dollars in the package exactly is the amount that immediately separates the demand from everyone wanting one to nobody wanting one.

Bill James suggested that the same should be true for baseball players. The minor leagues are filled with players who are just short of being valuable enough to play in the big leagues—maybe the big league position requires twenty dollars worth of skills, and these AAA players are offering only $19.90 worth. The idea, then, is that when Claudell, your aging 37-year-old left fielder, slips from offering $20.50 worth of offense to only $19.50, bam, he's out of there and one of these $19.90 minor leaguers gets called up.

Of course, it's not that simple, since it's impossible to be able to tell Claudell's value down to the penny. But the idea can still work—the idea being that when players slip from $29 worth of value to $25, they should keep their jobs almost all the time, but when they slip from $22 to $18, that's when they should lose their jobs almost all the time.

This study will let us know if that's really the case.

PHIL BIRNBAUM

Offensive Replacement Levels

by Clifford Blau

Bill James once suggested that if one studied the rate of return for regulars at different levels of offensive production, one could determine the amount of hitting needed for players to keep their jobs. This required performance Mr. James calls the sustenance level, and I call here the offensive replacement level. Determining the offensive replacement level at each position is important for several reasons. First, it is valuable to use in estimating the value of a player to his team, which is simply how much better he is than whomever his team could replace him with without giving up another player. Since regulars who produce at less than the offensive replacement level lose their jobs, it is obvious that teams believe that there are players readily available who perform at least at that level. Thus, the replacement level can be used for evaluating players in general, rather than considering what specific person would take over for a given player if he were replaced. Second, it is useful for comparing the relative importance of fielding at each position, at least as perceived by managers. Theoretically, one could determine a player's defensive value by examining at what point he loses playing time due to weak hitting (see Eddie Brinkman for an example).

The complete results of my study can be found in Table 2. Both the replacement level and average production for each position have the expected relationship, in that first basemen and left fielders have the highest replacement levels and averages, and shortstops and second basemen the lowest. For those not familiar with runs created per game, Table 1 lists some representative seasons showing conventional statistics along with the corresponding runs created per game.

Table 1.

TYPICAL BATTING LINES FOR EACH LEVEL OF OFFENSIVE PRODUCTION IN RUNS CREATED PER GAME

RC/G	NAME, YEAR	AB	H	2B	3B	HR	BB	SB	BA	SA
2.0	Larry Bowa, 1973	446	94	11	3	0	24	10	.211	.249
2.5	Craig Robinson, 1974	452	104	4	6	0	30	11	.230	.265
3.0	Mark Belanger, 1970	459	100	6	5	1	52	13	.218	.259
3.5	Mike Andrews, 1972	505	111	18	0	7	70	2	.220	.297
4.0	Jerry Remy, 1978	583	162	24	6	2	40	30	.278	.350
4.5	Bill Melton, 1974	495	120	17	0	21	59	3	.242	.404
5.0	Brooks Robinson, 1970	608	168	31	4	18	53	1	.276	.429
5.5	Rico Petrocelli, 1970	583	152	31	3	29	67	1	.261	.473
6.0	Bobby Murcer, 1973	616	187	29	2	22	50	5	.304	.464
6.5	Paul Molitor, 1979	584	188	27	16	9	48	33	.322	.469
7.0	George Brett, 1977	564	176	32	13	22	55	14	.312	.532

Methodology

The first step was to determine the regular at each position (except pitcher) for each major league team from 1969 to 1989. I did this using the *Baseball Encyclopedia*, generally choosing the player listed there as the regular as long as he had made at least 243 outs (about 9 games [9 × 27] worth, a full season being 18 games worth [18 × 9 players = 162 games]), although sometimes, especially with catchers, I might go as low as 189 outs (7 games). If there was no regular, then that position was not included in the study for that team and year. Next, using the statistics in *Total Baseball*, I determined the runs created per 27 outs (RC/G) for each regular for the years 1969 to 1988. I then noted if the player was a regular the next season at any position (or DH), even if he played several positions and could not be considered a regular at one position, such as Dick Allen in 1970. If he was traded and played regularly for his new team, he was considered to have kept his job. If he did not play regularly the following season due to injury, but returned to regular status the year after that, I counted him as keeping his job. However, if he never played regularly again, his last season was not included in the study. After I had all these data, I set up ranges of one-half or one runs created per 27 outs for each position. Then it was a simple matter of counting up the number of players in each category and the number who returned the following season.

Results

As you can see in Table 2, the rate of return varies greatly from position to position. The number under each position is the percentage of regulars who returned as regulars the following season. The number to the right is the number of regulars in each category. Boxes around two ranges indicate that the ranges were combined in the table (e.g., at first base there were 7 regulars between 2.0 and 3.0 runs created per game.

Table 2.
PERCENTAGE OF REGULARS WHO RETURNED AS REGULARS THE FOLLOWING SEASON

RC/G	FIRST BASE		SECOND BASE		SHORTSTOP		THIRD BASE	
< 2.0			0.0%	3	33.3%	15	0.0%	1
2.0-2.5	42.9%	7	50.0%	18	59.1%	44	0.0%	4
2.5-3.0			57.1%	49	68.1%	91	40.0%	20
3.0-3.5	40.0%	10	61.7%	81	78.7%	89	66.7%	39
3.5-4.0	48.4%	31	80.2%	86	78.4%	97	67.2%	61
4.0-4.5	63.0%	54	86.1%	72	88.9%	63	83.3%	84
4.5-5.0	78.6%	70	89.2%	65	100.0%	35	90.9%	66
5.0-5.5	87.3%	142	94.7%	76	100.0%	36	88.5%	104
5.5-6.0								
6.0-6.9	90.3%	93	100.0%	39	100.0%	16	100.0%	59
7.0+	98.7%	75					100.0%	44

RC/G	LEFT FIELD		CENTER FIELD		RIGHT FIELD		CATCHER	
< 2.0			25.0%	4	0%	1	0.0%	1
2.0-2.5	40.0%	10	33.3%	3	63.6%	11	45.0%	20
2.5-3.0			55.6%	18			46.9%	49
3.0-3.5	36.7%	30	55.9%	34	55.0%	20	62.2%	74
3.5-4.0	40.0%	30	66.2%	68	55.6%	36	70.3%	64
4.0-4.5	69.8%	63	67.7%	65	58.0%	69	67.7%	65
4.5-5.0	81.7%	71	89.5%	76	79.2%	77	79.2%	72
5.0-5.5	78.8%	66	93.9%	115	86.6%	67	91.4%	81
5.5-6.0	89.8%	59			86.8%	76		
6.0-6.9	94.7%	95	98.7%	76	100.0%	61	95.7%	46
7.0+	96.4%	56	96.8%	31	98.5%	67		

The rates did not generally vary much between leagues. I had supposed that the replacement level would be slightly higher in the National League, since the designated hitter allows American League teams to put a weak fielder at DH and put a good-field/no-hit player in his stead, but that wasn't the case. Bill James had theorized that there would be a range of one-half runs created per 27 outs where the replacement level would change sharply. However, that did not prove to be true. The rates tend to change slowly; in some cases, it was lower at a slightly higher level of production—e.g., at catcher, players hitting between 3.5 and 3.9 RC/G returned 70% of the time while at 4.0-4.4 RC/G, the rate of return was 68%. Note that although I studied a total of 504 team/seasons, the sample size in each range is fairly small.

The replacement level for each position is about 1.5 to 2 runs below average production. I expected it to be one run below, since using the Pythagorean method of predicting winning average, at the average level of 4.2 RC/G, 1 run below gives a winning average of .367, 1.5 below yields an average of .292, and 2 runs below average gives a result of .215. In the past I have used one run above average for pitchers, which seems superficially valid. Thus, the level for hitters shouldn't be so low for an average fielder. It may be that it is artificially lowered by only good fielders being allowed to play regularly at low levels of offense (e.g., the young Ozzie Smith), so the offensive replacement level for average fielders is actually higher than is shown on the chart.

In considering the validity of this study, one must consider several factors. One is that a single season's statistics may not accurately represent a player's ability—indeed, several players who kept their jobs after a poor season were established players having an off year and their teams obviously believed that they could do better the next year. Another is that other factors than offense are more important than I have hypothesized. Also: the overall level of offense varied during the period; a manager may overestimate a player's offense based on an incomplete understanding of statistics; finally, a team may not have an adequate replacement available and/or doesn't want to take a chance on an unproven player. Any of these factors could result in a "true" offensive replacement level being higher or lower than I have calculated.

Other Study

Another study of this question was done by Phil Birnbaum and published in *By the Numbers* in September, 1994. Phil used the entire 20th century as the basis for his study. Some differences in methodology included counting a player as returning if he ever played regularly again and counting all outfield positions together. He also tested the results when a player's Fielding Runs (as defined in *Total Baseball*) were taken into account. Both times the results were generally consistent with my findings: no clear replacement level but rather a gradual drop in return rate as hitting decreased.

This article originally appeared in the October 1998 issue of *By The Numbers*.

Introduction to "Finding Better Batting Orders"

Mark D. Pankin's work, of which this article is a prime example, typically employs what are known as "Markov process models," named in honor of mathematician Andrei Andreyevich Markov's pioneering work in this area. When we use these models, we think about the inning as a sequence of events called "base/out situations." There are twenty-five such situations, which can be identified as follows: the eight on-base possibilities (no runners, first only, second only, third only, first and second, first and third, second and third, and loaded) multiplied by the three out possibilities during a half inning (none, one, two), plus a twenty-fifth for the third out conclusion to the half inning. There are quite a few possible sequences through these events, although some are relatively rare (e.g., first and second/no out followed by three outs thanks to triple play). By running through these sequences, Markov models allow us to compute either the number of runs that would score on average, or, in contrast, the odds of scoring any runs at all, for each base-out situation. Then, by comparing these computations, we can determine whether various strategies are on average good or bad choices. For example, we have found that the stolen base is generally a good idea if the odds of success are about two-thirds or greater, that the normal sacrifice bunt is a good one-run strategy but poor overall (as an out loses much more than a base gains), that the intentional walk is almost always a mistake, that the hit-and-run is usually a good move, and that the suicide squeeze is a very good play when the bunter is sufficiently skilled (as a run is worth an out almost any day).

In the study published here, Mark Pankin has adapted the model for use in a more general strategic decision, the composition of the lineup. Basically, he computed the number of runs that a given lineup would score on average for each inning of a game, added those up to estimate the average number of runs the lineup would score in a game, and then compared these results for many different types of lineups. Many of his findings are consistent with other accepted results of sabermetric research.

A few observations:

The importance of on-base average to the number two batter's contribution is one more demonstration of the fallacy of the myth about "making contact and moving the runner along"; again, a base is not worth an out.

I was actually surprised to find that walking is not important in the fifth spot, given that number five is most likely to lead off the second inning.

And most important, the difference between the ideal lineup and the conventional one seems to work out to only one victory a year. In fact, the difference between the best and worst seems to mean only three victories a year. Other analyses of the same issue have reached the same general conclusion. Rather than agonizing all night about lineups, a manager would be better off getting some sleep and being alert for the next game.

Since this work, Mark has done analogous Markov studies of the impact of team speed, strikeouts, base advancement, and (his latest) the effect of stolen base attempts on the performance of subsequent batters.

CHARLIE PAVITT

Finding Better Batting Orders

By Mark D. Pankin

Given the nine starting players, in what order should they bat? Traditional guidelines such as "the leadoff man should be a good base stealer," "number two should be a contact hitter who can hit behind the runner," and "bat your best hitter third" abound. Due to computational complexities, there have been few studies that analyze the batting order question from a quantitative viewpoint. This article discusses what I believe is the most comprehensive mathematical and statistical approach to lineup determination. The models and the methods used to develop them are described, and some resulting principles of batting order construction are presented. Finally, the models are applied to the 1991 AL division winners and compared to the batting orders employed by the teams' managers.

The study utilizes two mathematical/statistical models:

1. A Markov process model that calculates the long-term average (often called expected) runs per game that a given lineup will score.
2. A statistically derived model that quantitatively evaluates the suitability of each of the nine players in each of the nine batting order positions. Data for the second model were generated by numerous runs of the Markov model. Hence, we see that the Markov model underlies the entire analysis.

The Markov Process Model

The Markov process model is based on the probabilities of moving from one runners and outs situation to another, possibly the same, situation. These probabilities, which depend on who is batting, are called transition probabilities. For example, one such transition is from no one on and no outs to a runner on first and no outs; and the transition probabilities are that of a single, walk, hit batsman, safe at first on an error, catcher interference, or striking out and reaching first on a wild pitch or passed ball. The Markov model employs matrix algebra to perform the complex calculations. However, once all the requisite probabilities have been determined, the matrix formulation enables the remaining calculations to be carried out without much difficulty.

It is important to note that assumptions made in determining the transition probabilities have an enormous influence on the the batting order results presented later. The goal is to choose a realistic set of assumptions, but, as always, some simplifying assumptions are quite helpful. Moreover, some of the assumptions are open to alternatives, the particular ones employed being a matter of judgment or study objectives. The key assumptions for the current analysis are:

1. Players bat the same in all situations. For this study, each player's 1990 full season data were used to determine how he would bat.
2. All base advancement, outs on the bases (including double plays), wild pitches, passed balls, balks, etc., occur according to major league average probabilities.
3. Stolen base attempts are permitted with a runner on first only.

4. Only pitchers attempt sacrifice bunts.
5. Overall 1990 pitcher batting is used for all pitchers.
6. Small adjustments to hit and walk frequencies are made in certain situations. In particular, there are more walks and fewer hits when there are runners on base and first base is not occupied.

Data for #2 and #6 are derived from combined AL and NL data for the 1986 season. The first assumption is the most critical and most controversial. One of its consequences is that the differences in expected runs between batting orders tend to be relatively small. A previous, less extensive study that incorporated situational performance assumptions (e.g., certain players hit better with runners on) showed much larger differences in expected scoring. I plan to explore various alternative assumptions about performance levels in future batting order studies.

Base advancement on hits certainly is not uniform, since it depends on runner speed and where the particular batter tends to get his hits (e.g., the percentage of singles to left, center, or right). However, I did not have the data needed to incorporate such effects. Data availability also prevented batter-specific double play modeling.

The stolen base try restriction does not have a large effect because over 80% of steal attempts occur with a runner on first only. The restriction to this case greatly simplifies the computations and is not likely to affect comparisons between batting orders. Sacrifice bunt tries are not included for non-pitchers because they are game situation-specific and reduce overall scoring, contrary to the study objective of finding the highest scoring lineups.

Data for the Statistical Models

The Markov model was used for two primary purposes. One is to evaluate a specific batting order by calculating its expected runs per game. In this way, alternative lineups can be compared. The second purpose is the generation of data for use in the statistical models. For each of the 26 major league teams in 1990, 200 "batting rotations" were chosen at random. A batting rotation consists in specifying the order in which the players will bat by establishing who follows whom, but a rotation does not become a lineup or batting order until the leadoff hitter in the first inning is specified. Each batting rotation corresponds to nine lineups, one for each possible leadoff batter. The Markov calculations have the property that the computations needed for one lineup are also sufficient for the other eight lineups corresponding to the same batting rotation. There is nothing special about the choice of 200; it was a function of the computing power available to me and the amount of time I could spend on this phase of the study. More, as usually is the case for statistical analyses, would have been better.

Thus, the Markov model computed the expected runs per game for 1,800 "semi-randomly" (a made-up concept, since only the batting rotations are chosen at random) generated batting orders incorporating the nine most frequent players, one for each position. One property of the 1,800 lineups is that each of the nine players hits in each batting position exactly 200 times.

The next step was to select the best lineups for each team from the 1,800 tested. I used two definitions of best. The first is obvious: select the ones with the highest expected runs per game. The second definition is more subtle. Each batting rotation will have one lineup that scores the best, and this lineup may or may not be one of the highest scoring lineups out of the 1,800. Call the highest scoring lineup for each rotation a *maximal* lineup. The reason a maximal lineup, which may not be a particularly high scoring lineup overall, is of interest is that it can reveal advantages to batting certain players in certain positions although the overall scoring is held down by the batting positions of other players. Since there were 200 maximal lineups, one for each rotation, I decided to use them and the 200 highest-scoring lineups as the basis for the statistical analysis. I did not determine how many of the maximal lineups were also in the 200 highest scoring.

Within each set of 200 best lineups, I computed how often each player hit in each batting position. For example, Wade Boggs leads off in 21% of Boston's highest-scoring lineups. (This value, the highest on the team, means that Boggs is a good first hitter since the average is 100%/9 = 11.1%) In this way, each player has a rating for his suitability for each batting order position.

For each player I computed scores in 21 offensive measures *relative* to the group of nine starting players on his team. The offensive measures are batting average; on-base average; slugging average; slugging average modified by counting walks as singles and SF as AB (which is the relationship of on-base percentage to batting average); extra base average ($=SA-BA$, also called isolated power); runs created per game; frequency per plate appearance of each type of hit, walks (including hit by pitch), and strikeouts; relative frequency of each type of hit (i.e., the percentage of players hits that are singles, doubles, etc.); percentage of plate appearances that are not walks or strikeouts (which measures putting the ball in play); secondary average $[=(TB-H+BB+SB-CS)/AB$, a Bill James idea]; run element ratio $[=(BB+SB)/(TB-H)$, another Bill James idea]; steal attempt frequency $[=(SB+CS)/(1B+BB)]$; and stolen base success percentage. No claim is made that the set of measures chosen is complete or perfect, just that it covers all the significant aspects of offensive performance.

I used two measures of player performance relative to the team: 1) percentage above or below the team mean in the category, and 2) the z-score, which is the number of standard deviations above or below the mean. By using z-scores, I am not claiming any of these distributions is normal (given that there are only nine values for a team in each offensive category, the distributions are almost certainly not even approximately normal); I am just using z-scores as a measure of relative performance.

Regression Analysis

In the next phase, I applied regression analysis using the players' batting position ratings (e.g., Wade Boggs' 21% batting first) as the dependent variable and their relative scores for the various offensive measures as the candidate independent variables. For each batting position there are 236 data points—one for each of the nine players on the 26 teams—used in the regression estimates. Because there were two measures for batting position ratings (one based on the highest-scoring lineups and one based on the maximal lineups) and two measures of relative offensive performance (percentages above or below the team mean and z-scores), there are four possible categories of models that can be derived. I tested all four, as described below, decided on the one that seemed to yield the models with the best statistical properties, and focused on that one. The best combination from the first round of testing was highest-scoring rather than maximal lineups as the basis of the dependant variable and z-scores for the independent variables.

To do the regressions, I used the stepwise regression procedure in the SHAZAM statistical package with a 10% significance level required for variables to enter or leave the equations. One equation is estimated for each batting order position, and the estimates are done independently. Since the nine batting position values for a given player must add to 100%, I experimented with some joint estimation techniques. However, they did not yield significantly different models from the independent estimates, so I used the independent estimates throughout this study. After performing stepwise regressions for each of the four categories of models described in the previous paragraph, I restricted further investigation to the highest-scoring/z-scores category.

For this first set of regressions for highest-scoring/z-scores models, the r^2 values range from a high of 0.914 (#9 position) to a low of 0.580 (#6). It is no surprise that the best fit is obtained for the #9 position because of the inclusion of NL teams with pitchers that bat. The number of independent variables in these equations range from a low of 4 (#2,#4) to 12 (#9). Overall, I judged this to be good and workable set of models. Three candidate variables—home runs per plate appearance, run element ratio, and stolen base success percentage (which is highly correlated with steal attempt frequency)—did not enter any of the nine model equations. The variables most frequently in the equations were runs created per game (in seven equations, all but #4 and #5) and modified slugging average including walks (in six, all but #2, #5, #7).

The offensive performance measures that are the basis of the independent variables are not truly independent, and several measure similar player performance characteristics. Since the models usually included several such variables, often with opposite signs, I decided to see if a smaller set of independent variables could yield models with r^2 values almost as high, but which lend themselves to more sensible interpretations. After examining the equations and the correlation matrix of the candidate independent variables, I restricted the candidates to the following nine: on base average (OBA), slugging average (SA), extra base average (EBA), BB/PA, K/PA, 1B/H, HR/H, ball in play percentage (INPLAY), steal attempt frequency (SBTRY).

Table 1. Variables in Order of Importance

POS	1	2	3	4	5	6	7
1	+OBA	+BB/PA	-INPLAY	-HR/H	-SBTRY		
2	+SLUG	+OBA	-EBA	+BB/PA	-INPLAY		
3	+SLUG	+BB/PA	+INPLAY				
4	+SLUG	+OBA	-HR/H				
5	+SLUG	-HR/H	+INPLAY	+SBTRY			
6	-RC/G	+SLUG	+INPLAY	+OBA	+K/PA	+SBTRY	
7	-OBA	+INPLAY	+SBTRY				
8	-SLUG	-OBA	-BB/PA	+HR/H	+INPLAY		
9	-INPLAY	-K/PA	-SLUG	-OBA	-BB/PA	+1B/H	-SBTRY

The resulting set of models had r^2 values from 0.885 (#9) down to 0.607 (#5) and 0.434 (#6). With the exception of #6, the decline in r^2 is not a major concern. In order to improve the model for the sixth position, I added RC/G to the set of candidate independent variables for that equation only, which improved its r^2 to 0.557. The number of independent variables ranges from 3 (#3,#4,#7) to 7 (#9). Each candidate variable appeared in at least one of the model equations. Table 1 summarizes the models; a plus sign before the variable means high scores are best for the particular batting order position, and a minus sign indicates the opposite. There are numerical values, the model equation parameters, which are not shown, associated with each variable in the table. These values determine the relative importance of the variables.

I also did some regression analyses using each of the leagues separately because I wanted to see if the DH rule affected the models. In general, the statistical properties—goodness of fit and significance levels of the parameters—were poorer for the models based on the separate leagues. Also, I was not able to interpret the models in a way that could answer the DH question. I suspect that I need more and better data to do this analysis. More in that teams from seasons other than 1990 should be included, and better in that more than 200 batting rotations should be calculated to determine the player/batting position scores. Additional candidate independent variables should also be considered. Due to time constraints, I did not pursue these models further, but this is a topic worth further investigation if for no other reason than the feeling of some AL managers that the number nine hitter should considered a second leadoff hitter.

Generating Lineups Based on the Batting Position Models

Once the batting position model equations are in hand for a given team, we can compute a value in each of the nine batting order positions for each player. These values can be positive, meaning the player is better than average for the particular lineup position, or negative, which has the opposite meaning. These scores serve to rank the nine players for each lineup position and also to identify the best position for each player. The next step is using those values to find one or more high-scoring lineups. Things would be easy if the best position for each player was the highest rating for that position on the entire team. This occurs, for example, if Wade Boggs best spot is leadoff and the highest-scoring leadoff man on the Red Sox is Boggs; Jody Reed's best spot is #2 and the Sox's best #2 is Reed; etc. However, such is rarely the case. Due to the nature of the models, it is common for the player with the best leadoff score to also have the best #2 score and a high #3 score. Also, the scores on the ends of the lineup (#1, #2, #8, #9) tend to be more extreme, both on the high and low sides, than the scores in the middle. This reflects the models' emphasis on the importance of having high on-base average hitters at the top of the order, which is discussed later.

What we need is a method of assigning players to lineup positions so that total model scores from the assignments is high. This is a well-known operations research topic known as an *assignment problem*. Fortunately, this type of problem can be solved using several methods, some of which are easy to implement on computers and run quickly. I chose an algorithm that not only finds the best possible assignment, but also finds the top *n* assignments, where *n* can be specified. For the purposes of this study, I set *n* equal to five. For each set of batting positions models—one based on the full set of independent variables and one based on the reduced set—I found the five highest assignments for a team, which were always quite close in total batting position values. These lineups were fed into the Markov model to find the expected runs per game. The lineup with the highest expected scoring was usually one of the top three solutions to the assignment problem, but the best solution did not seem to have an advantage over the next two. In some cases, a comparison of the expected scoring and the batting order differences among lineups led me to formulate a lineup with even better expected runs per game that was not in the five solutions to the assignment problem.

For each of the 1990 major league teams, I compared the expected runs of the best lineups found using the models described in the table with the best found using the models based on the full set of candidate independent variables. For three AL and six NL teams, the full-variable models had a slight advantage (about 1-2 runs a season), and for four AL and two NL teams, the reduced-variable set models had a similar advantage. For the rest of the teams, the two sets of models were virtually the same. Because the smaller variable-set models are easier to comprehend, the discussion in the next section is based on those models.

Interpreting the Models

Due to the nature of the regression process, it can be misleading to draw conclusions about individual variables without considering the context provided by the entire set of variables. One example is the -SBTRY for the leadoff position. This is the fifth most important variable (its weight is about 10% that of OBA, which is by far and away the most important characteristic of a good leadoff hitter). Even so, does it mean that other things being equal, which they never are, it is better to have a leadoff hitter who doesn't try to steal? It might, but it also may just be the regression distinguishing certain slow effective leadoff hitters based on the Markov model—Wade Boggs, for example. Additional statistical analysis, which I have not yet gotten to, could determine if one or two specific players are the cause of the -SBTRY.

The less important explanatory variables often play a role of emphasizing or modifying the more important ones. For example, the -INPLAY in the #1 and #2 positions serves to emphasize BB/PA. If I wanted to try to find the best set of variables for each position, I would try to build these two models without INPLAY. To illustrate the idea of modification, the -EBA in #2 balances the +SLUG and +OBA. Often players with high OBA have high BA and above-average SLUG, since slugging average incorporates batting average. The negative EBA in effect puts more weight on the OBA and less weight on power. A more interesting instance is the -HR/H in the model for #4. Does this mean that the cleanup hitter shouldn't hit homers? No, what it means is that among players with high slugging averages, it is better to have one who does not get his slugging average mainly from home runs—a Dave Kingman—but instead has a good batting average and hits a fair number of doubles—an Eddie Murray.

The model equations, which are not shown, can be interpreted to characterize the desirable abilities for each batting order position:

1. Getting on base is everything. To much lesser extent, home run hitters should not lead off. Stolen base ability is irrelevant.
2. Similar to the leadoff hitter, but not quite as crucial to get on base; some power is also desirable.
3. Should have fair power, be able to draw walks, and not strike out much.
4. Highest slugging average; also has a good on-base percentage and is not necessarily the best home run hitter.
5. Good power; secondarily puts ball in play (i.e., does not walk or strike out a lot).
6. Hardest spot to characterize and probably least critical. Probably want to use player who doesn't fit well in other positions. Base stealing ability is a small plus.
7-9. Decreasing overall abilities as hitters as characterized by on-base percentage and measures of power hitting.

One clear result from this and prior studies is the importance of having the right batters at the top of the order. This follows from the finding that most of the difference in expected runs between high- and low-scoring lineups using the same players occurs in the first inning. In particular, the leadoff batter must have a high on-base percentage. Also, the second hitter must be good. The practice of leading off a fast runner who can steal bases but doesn't get on base much, and putting a weak hitter "with good bat control who can bunt or hit behind the runner" second is a perfect prescription for a lower-scoring batting order.

Applying the Models

To see them in action, consider what these models say about the 1991 ALCS teams, Toronto and Minnesota. Batter performance is based on full-season 1991 data, and no righty-lefty splits are used. The lineups used by the teams were against right-handed starting pitchers. Before Joe Carter was hurt in game three, Cito Gaston used the batting order: 1) D. White, 2) R. Alomar, 3) J. Carter, 4) J. Olerud, 5) K. Gruber, 6) C. Maldonado, 7) L. Mulliniks, 8) P. Borders, 9) M. Lee.

The Markov model expected runs per game for this lineup is 4.739. This value is about 0.5 higher than Toronto's 1991 actual of 4.222 runs per game. That the Markov values are higher than the actual is to be expected for several reasons. The most important are: 1) the players listed are generally better than the substitutes who play for various reasons; 2) sacrifice bunt attempts, which decrease overall scoring, are not included in the Markov model; 3) relief pitchers brought in with men on base or to face particular hitters can reduce late-inning scoring; and 4) a good team usually loses more innings in games won at home than it gains in extra-inning games, but the Markov value is based on nine complete innings per game.

The highest scoring lineup found by the models is: 1) Mulliniks, 2) Olerud, 3) Maldonado, 4) White, 5) Alomar, 6) Carter, 7) Gruber, 8) Borders, 9) Lee.

The Markov value for the above lineup is 4.795 runs per game, which is about 9 runs per 162-game season more than Gaston's, a difference that should be worth one extra win. (Keep in mind that differences in expected runs between lineups are small due to the assumption that each player's batting is the same in all situations.)

Mulliniks should lead off because he has an on-base average (OBA) of .364, the highest in this group, and little power. White, in contrast, has an OBA of .342 and the second best slugging average (.455, Carter's is .503), so he should not lead off despite his stolen base ability. The major surprise is that Carter bats sixth. The batting position equations score him as best on the team in the third, fourth, and fifth spots, but Maldonado, White, and Alomar rate so low as sixth that Carter is put there instead. Tests using the Markov model showed it makes virtually no difference if Carter bats fourth and White and Alomar fill the five and six slots in either order.

Minnesota's Tom Kelly employed the following order in the four games against right-handed starters: 1) D. Gladden, 2) C. Knoblauch, 3) K. Puckett, 4) K. Hrbek, 5) C. Davis, 6) B. Harper, 7) S. Mack, 8) M. Pagliarulo, 9) G. Gagne.

The Markov process expected runs per game is 5.383 for this lineup, which is higher than the Twins' 1991 average of 4.790 for the reasons given previously. The best model-generated lineup is: 1) Hrbek, 2) Davis, 3) Mack, 4) Puckett, 5) Harper, 6) Gagne, 7) Gladden, 8) Pagliarulo, 9) Knoblauch.

The Markov value of the model lineup is 5.431, about 8 runs higher than Kelly's, which might yield one more victory. Clearly, the model result flies in the face of "conventional wisdom," but one reason for building models is to gain new knowledge. Perhaps the best thing is getting Gladden out of the leadoff spot because his 1991 OBA of .306 is by far the worst among the nine players. I never cease to be amazed by managers who are so fascinated by speed that they forget players can't steal first base! Davis and Hrbek have the two highest OBAs, and the model takes advantage of this by loading the top part of the order. One reason Davis with a slugging average of .507 can bat second is that Mack's at .529 is even better. Knoblauch is an interesting case because the model values him highest at either the top or bottom of the order. However, on this team he is best suited to the bottom because his OBA is far from the best.

One important factor not considered is what assumptions, if any, the managers make about batting performance by their players. If I knew such, those levels could be put into the models, and then we could judge better how well the managers constructed their batting orders.

Those with computer baseball games that will automatically play hundreds or thousands of games may find it interesting to enter the 1991 data for these two teams and then compare the scoring of the lineups shown above for a large number of games. I would be interested in seeing how the results of the simulations compare with the Markov calculations.

Table 2. ADVANTAGE IN EXPECTED RUNS OF MODEL OVER MANAGERS

RUNS/GAME	APPROXIMATE RUNS PER 162 GAMES	AL	NL
.095 - .105	16	1 (CHI)	
.085 - .095			
.075 - .085	13		1 (PHI)
.065 - .075	11	1	2
.055 - .065	9.5	2	1
.045 - .055	8	4	2
.035 - .045	6.5	1	2
.025 - .035	5	1	3
.015 - .025	3.25	2	
.005 - .015			
-.005 - .005	0	2 (BOS, MIL)	1 (SF)

As a test of how well the models work, I compared lineups found by the models with lineups used by the teams in 1990. For each team I tabulated the number of times each player started a game in each batting order position. From this information I constructed one or more typical lineups for each team. Some teams did not really have anything close to a set lineup, and others platooned certain fielding and batting order positions. In all cases, I developed batting orders that were typical of those used by the managers and that reflect their thinking. Using the Markov process expected runs calculations, I compared the best team lineup with the best lineup found by either of the two sets of models—one using all the candidate independent variables and one using the reduced variable set described above. The table shows the extent to which the model did better than the major league managers.

A general rule of thumb is that an additional 10 runs a season leads to one more win. We see that the model lineups were better than the managers' in 23 of 26 cases with the other three being virtually equal. These comparisons are far from definitive because the models are based on the assumptions listed previously. Also, managers consider many factors when deciding on batting orders, some of which can't be modeled. For example, although Barry Bonds would be an outstanding leadoff hitter because he gets on base so much, according to an article in August 12, 1991 *Sporting News* he prefers to bat fifth where he can get more RBIs and hence more attention and presumably a higher salary. Even if he has faith in my models, Jim Leyland might figure that a happy Bonds hitting fifth can help his team more than an unhappy Bonds leading off. Moreover, Bonds might not draw so many walks if he were batting first.

Conclusion

Although I believe this study is a major advance of our knowledge about batting orders, the models discussed are not intended to be the final word on the subject. In particular, incorporation of some situational batting effects should be considered. One, of particular interest, is how the strength or weakness of the next hitter(s) affects a player's batting performance. For example, is there really a tendency to pitch around a strong hitter if he is followed by a weak one? The primary problem is obtaining relevant data. Also, there is room for improvement in the statistical (regression) modeling process; additional candidate independent variables should be studied.

This article originally appeared in the December 1991 issue of *By The Numbers*.

Introduction to "What Drives MVP Voting?"

Some years it seems so easy. Other years it provokes more debate than the Florida voting system. For more than seven decades now, the baseball writers of America have been choosing MVPs. Which means that, for every one of those seven decades, people have been wrestling with a question that ought to be simple in theory:

What does the term "most valuable player" really mean?

There are more opinions than there are candidates. But thankfully, Rob Wood provides us with this detailed, comprehensive study of the history of MVP voting to break down which statistics and other factors have held the most significance for the voters themselves.

The 2002 American League MVP debate was the perfect example of just how confusing this entire process can be. There was nearly unanimous agreement that Texas's Alex Rodriguez was the best player in the American League. Obviously, Rodriguez had the best pure numbers, leading the league in home runs and RBIs while having the greatest offensive season of any shortstop in history. But ARod compiled those numbers for a last-place team. So voters were left to struggle with the question of whether the best players on the four playoff teams—Oakland's Miguel Tejada, Anaheim's Garret Anderson, Minnesota's Torii Hunter, and the Yankees' two most dominant players, Alfonso Soriano and Jason Giambi—were more "valuable" than ARod.

Even many of the voters themselves seemed confused as the deadline neared for casting those ballots. So they were forced to look at history to see how the voters before them defined the word "valuable."

Wood's study shows us how much weight previous voters have placed on where candidates' teams finished, at just how wide a margin by which MVPs from first-place teams outnumbered MVPs from also-rans. He also examines the 1998 MVP race between Sammy Sosa and Mark McGwire and speculates, with great vision, about the future impact of the wild card on MVP voting.

When a race is close, voters often wonder which statistics ought to carry the most weight, and it is natural that they look to see which statistics carried the most weight in the past. If a player leads the league in RBIs, has that historically been worth more than being a home run champ or winning a batting title? Wood provides us with charts that answer those questions more clearly than ever.

Yet even with all this data, several winners—and losers —over the years have defied the traditional definitions and trends. Wood looks at those, too, and analyzes why the models don't always work. It all comes back to the original great debate: What *is* a "most valuable player?" All of us who have held a ballot in our hands—and many who haven't—know that *everyone* has his or her own idea of how to answer that question. There's no right answer. There's no wrong answer. But history provides a telltale guide to how most voters have answered. And Rob Wood has given us an invaluable study of that history.

JAYSON STARK

What Drives MVP Voting?

by Rob Wood

Introduction

The 1998 league MVP awards went to players that had very good credentials, but still caused some consternation in several quarters. Sammy Sosa beat out Mark McGwire by a wide margin (30 to 2 first-place votes) in the NL, and Juan Gonzalez beat out a good crop of candidates in the AL.

As you know, Sosa led the league in total bases, runs scored, and runs batted in. McGwire led the league in home runs (no kidding), walks, on-base average, and slugging percentage, not to mention most of the sabermetric measures such as runs created and total player rating. Of course, the Cubs made the playoffs via the wild card while the Cardinals did not.

Do not think that controversial MVP awards are a modern phenomenon. Alas, the history of baseball is sprinkled with surprising MVP awards. To name but a few: Frank McCormick in 1940, DiMaggio over Williams in 1947, Hank Sauer in 1952, Yogi Berra in 1954, Elston Howard in 1963, Zoilo Versalles in 1965, Roberto Clemente in 1966, Boog Powell in 1970, Don Baylor in 1979, Andre Dawson in 1987, Robin Yount in 1989, Barry Larkin in 1995.

In this article, I do not want to focus on any specific MVP injustices, though clearly McGwire would have received my vote. Instead, I hope to analyze past voting to see if we can determine what actually drives MVP balloting. In particular we can test whether leading the league in RBI, as Sosa and Gonzalez did, actually has the largest impact as many people believe. By so doing, we will be able to better understand what the voters think "Most Valuable Player" really means.

I have compiled a database of each of the 67 seasons' complete MVP balloting by the BBWAA from 1931 to 1998. Following tradition, I use a player's MVP award share as the data we are attempting to understand. Award share is the fraction of all possible points that a player receives, where the maximum is 1.00 if he is a unanimous MVP (i.e., received all the first-place votes). I am not sure how the votes were cast and tallied over the years, but currently a player receives 14 points for a first-place vote, 9 points for a second-place vote, 8 for 3rd, 7 for 4th, down to 1 point for a 10th-place vote. Using award shares is necessary for historical analysis as the number of voters, and thus the raw number of MVP points, has changed over the years.

Award shares range from 0 to 1. The average award share across all the 134 league MVPs is .85. The highest award share of 1.00, of course, was received by the 13 unanimous MVP winners (Greenberg 1935, Rosen 1953, Mantle 1956, Robinson 1966, Cepeda 1967, McLain 1968, Jackson 1973, Schmidt 1980, Canseco 1988, Thomas 1993, Bagwell 1994, Caminiti 1996, Griffey 1997). The lowest award share received by an AL MVP was .55 by Yogi Berra in 1951, and the lowest by an NL MVP was .57 by Marty Marion in 1944.

The "explanatory" variables that I will use to try to explain MVP award shares are the league leaders in offensive categories, as well as where the team finished in the standings. The analysis will be purposefully coarse as I am not attempting to determine who actually deserved each MVP, but the underlying reasons why the player won. For example, I will not use any measure other than leading the league, so finishing second in a category gives you no credit in my model. This is admittedly crude, but I want to first get an idea of what is driving things. Subsequent research could expand and/or refine my model.

League Leaders

Let's first take a look at the raw data. Table 1 reports how the league leader in the offensive categories fared in that season's MVP balloting. You can see that I include all of the traditional offensive categories and several of the new sabermetric categories. The table is ordered by how often the MVP winner led in each offensive category.

The first row of the table indicates that the player who led the league in RBI won the MVP 38% of the time, finished in the top three in MVP balloting 64% of the time, finished in the top five 77% of the time, and garnered an average MVP award share of .58.

The only variable that may need explanation is Total Player Rating. This is Pete Palmer's Total Player Rating (TPR) among hitters only, denoting the player who contributed the most wins to his team using Pete's linear weights formulas for hitting, base running, and fielding. For the purposes of Table 1, if there was a tie for the league leadership in an offensive category, among those players tied the player who received the highest award share was used.

The table of league leaders' MVP showing within each league looks remarkably similar. Indeed, I have not identified any significant differences between the two leagues' MVP balloting. Throughout the article, all data and results pertain to both the AL and NL (i.e., the combined dataset of 134 league-seasons).

For comparison to the percentages listed in the table, the MVP winner played on a team who finished first 68% of the time. Thus, about twice as often as the MVP was the RBI league leader, the MVP played on a first-place team. Of course, many players play on a first-place team, and divisional play has spawned multiple first-place teams. Thus, it is not obvious who on the first-place team will receive all the "credit" for finishing first. We will come back to this issue below.

All data used in this article is from the Bill James/STATS Inc. *All-Time Baseball Sourcebook* published in 1998. In this great book James and STATS have slightly reworked the runs-created formulas, and thus have some new league leaders in runs created than previously published. I use their designated league leader for all of the offensive categories.

The table below shows that RBI does indeed lead the parade. But "only" 38% of the time does the league leader in RBI win the MVP. RBI is followed fairly closely by Total Player Rating, Runs Created, Slugging Percentage, and On-Base Average Plus Slugging Percentage. We next try to make sense of the data.

Table 1. LEAGUE LEADERS AND THE MVP (1931-1998 AL & NL)

	WON MVP (%)	TOP 3 IN MVP (%)	TOP 5 IN MVP (%)	AVERAGE AWARD SHARE
RBI	38	64	77	.58
TPR	35	52	66	.52
RC	33	63	80	.58
SLG	32	61	76	.57
OBA + SLG	32	61	73	.55
TOTAL BASES	29	65	84	.58
RC/27	29	59	75	.55
HR	26	57	73	.53
R	23	46	65	.45
BA	18	47	58	.43
OBA	18	35	48	.38
H	11	42	57	.40
2B	10	27	41	.30
BB	8	21	35	.25
3B	7	18	25	.19
SB	4	9	15	.12

MVP Model Data

Table 1 merely listed the number of times that the MVP led the league in various offensive categories. While this is a first step, it does not tell us what really drives MVP balloting. Of course, in many years one player leads the league in multiple offensive categories. We want to identify which categories are the true drivers and which are merely along for the ride.

I use the entire history of BBWAA MVP balloting in order to ensure that the data is sufficiently rich. We need varied data to help us sort out true effects from spurious effects. Several characteristics of the dataset are desirable. First, the data should exhibit a wide range of quality of players to lead the league in each offensive category. If so, a true measure of the impact of leading the league can be estimated. The alternative is a case in which a "Babe Ruth" leads the league in a category every year and wins the MVP; did Babe win the MVP because he led the league or because he is the Babe?

While most league leaders in most offensive categories merit some degree of MVP consideration, over the years some fairly nondescript players have been league leaders. The following litany probably deserved and received only scant MVP voting for leading their league: Ivan DeJesus (runs 1978), Garry Templeton (hits 1979), Mike Hargrove (walks 1978), Matty Alou (doubles 1969), Mariano Duncan (triples, 1990), Dave Kingman (home runs 1982), Reggie Smith (total bases 1971), Larry Hisle (RBI 1977), Willie Wilson (batting average 1982), Vince Coleman (stolen bases, many years), Darrell Evans (runs created 1973), Alvin Davis (runs created per 27 outs), Kal Daniels (on base average 1988), Harold Baines (slugging percentage 1984), and Roy Smalley (total player rating 1979). The point is that over the entire history of BBWAA MVP voting, we have seen a wide variety of the quality of league leaders in virtually every offensive category. The analysis that follows will attempt to sift through all the data to uncover accurate estimates of the impact of leading the league on MVP voters.

Second, the impact of a few players should be minimized. Suppose a hypothetical player, call him Paul Bunyan, won the MVP many times. Then the offensive characteristics of Paul Bunyan could dominate the MVP impact estimates. For example, if

Bunyan led the league each year in triples, as well as home runs, RBIs, etc., then our model could tell us that leading the league in triples was important to MVP voters. Over the course of 67 years, the impact of any individual is minimized. And no players have ever won more than three MVP awards (those with three are Foxx, DiMaggio, Berra, Mantle, Musial, Campanella, Schmidt, and Bonds).

Third, the data should be sufficiently rich and varied so as to not exhibit multi-collinearity. This means that over the course of the history, the league leaders in two or more categories do not overlap too much. For example, suppose that the league leader in home runs is virtually always also the league leader in total bases. Then, the model would not be able to separate out these two impacts. Fortunately, the 134 league-seasons of data are sufficient to mitigate against multicollinearity. In the database, the offensive categories paired by league leaders the most were RC/27out and OBA+SLG (107 times), SLG and OBA+SLG (100 times), and RC and RC/27out (93 times). Among the traditional categories, the same player led the league in both home runs and slugging percentage 71 times and both home runs and RBI 70 times.

MVP Model Estimation

Now that we are satisfied that the database is sufficiently rich and varied to permit analysis, let's turn to our model and its estimation. Since award shares are necessarily between 0 and 1, a standard linear regression is not appropriate. This is a reflection of the fact that the award share relationship is non-linear. Leading the league in multiple categories (in the extreme, all categories) exhibits diminishing returns in terms of award share. If a player leads the league in HR, RBI, and batting average, also leading the league in hits or runs will not add much to his award share. But a player who leads the league in only one category will get the full benefit.

I used a transformation to ensure that the model predictions are between 0 and 1. In particular, I used a log-linear transformation based upon the cumulative distribution function of the standard exponential distribution: $F(x) = 1-e^{-x}$. This function starts at 0 and climbs gradually up to 1 as x increases from 0 to infinity.

The model we estimate is

$$\text{SHARE} = 1 - \exp[-(C_1 \times L_1 + C_2 \times L_2 + \ldots + C_N \times L_N)]$$

where the L_i's are the explanatory variables, described below, and the C_i's are the coefficients we are attempting to estimate. All of the explanatory variables are dummy variables, taking on value 1 if true and 0 otherwise, and are listed in the table below.

Besides the league-leading variables, I have included variables for team finishes: first place (either division or league), making the playoffs but not finishing first (i.e., wild card or losing a tie-breaking series or game), and second place (either division or league). In order to make the model manageable, I parcelled out these team finishes' credits to three or fewer players on each team. In most years only one or two players is held responsible for a team's success, either rightly or wrongly. I have attempted to mimic this in these variables.

A regression analysis can be used to estimate the C's since the model can be transformed to a standard linear model via a logarithmic transformation yielding:

$$\text{LOG}[1/(1\text{-}\text{SHARE})] = C_1 \times L_1 + C_2 \times L_2 + \ldots + C_N \times L_N.$$

Of course, our goal is to estimate how much leading the league in each offensive category contributes to MVP award share. Clearly the C's are not directly that answer. Since we are using a log-linear model, we need to transform our coefficients (C's) into award share weights (W's). The transformation, as indicated by the original model, is given by $W_i = 1 - \exp(-C_i)$.

Table 2 presents two sets of estimates. The first pertains to a "traditional" model in which the sabermetric variables are excluded. The second pertains to the comprehensive model, which includes all traditional and sabermetric variables. For both models, the "raw" coefficient (C_i) is listed along with the transformed award share weight (W_i). The analysis was constrained to produce non-negative coefficients and weights.

In presenting the two model estimates, I am not suggesting that voters actually look at the new sabermetric league leaders, but rather that the sabermetric variables may reflect performances not captured in other variables. For the remainder of the article I will use the "traditional" model.

Table 2. MODEL COEFFICIENTS AND WEIGHTS

	(No Variables)		(Sabermetric Variables)	
	COEFFICIENT	SHARE WT.	COEFFICIENT	SHARE WT.
RBI	.84	.57	.83	.56
FINISHED 1ST*	.75	.53	.74	.52
SLG	.56	.43	.36	.30
FINISHED "1.5ST†	.42	.34	.43	.35
RC			.31	.27
R	.37	.31	.30	.26
TPR			.30	.26
TOTAL BASES	.30	.26	.22	.20
BA	.26	.23	.22	.19
FINISHED 2ND*	.18	.17	.17	.16
HR	.12	.12	.10	.09
OBA	.11	.10	.08	.00
H	.10	.10	.09	.09
RC/27			.04	.04
OBA + SLG			.03	.03
SB	.02	.01	.00	.00
2B	.00	.00	.00	.00
3B	.00	.00	.00	.00
BB	.00	.00	.00	.00

* At most three players receive this credit per team; "1.5" refers to tieing for first place and then losing a playoff or winning a wild card.

The table indicates that leading the league in RBI is the most important MVP award share variable. The raw coefficient of .84 translates into receiving an award share of .57. Coming in first place, and being one of the recipients for the credit, has a raw coefficient of .75, which translates into an award share of .53.

Let's use these two examples to demonstrate how to combine variables. Of course, we cannot simply add their award share weights. For one thing, .57 plus .53 exceeds 1.00, the maximum possible. And second, we explicitly developed a non-linear model precisely since we knew that the underlying relationship is non-linear. To find the estimated award share of a player who leads the league in RBI and whose team finished first is to add the raw coefficients, and then convert the sum via an exponential transformation. This method is used no matter how many offensive categories the player leads the league in.

Table 3. CONVERSION OF COEFFICIENTS TO SHARES (SHARE = 1-EXP(-SUM OF COEFFICIENTS)

					SUM OF COEFFICIENTS						
.00	.20	.40	.60	.80	1.00	1.50	2.00	2.50	3.00	3.50	4.00
.00	.18	.33	.45	.55	.63	.78	.86	.92	.95	.97	.98

PREDICTED MVP SHARE

Table 3 presents a table of conversions for reference. To complete the example of a RBI leader who finished first, add the raw coefficients .84 plus .75 to yield 1.59. Either by looking at Table 3 or doing the exponential transformation (1-exp(-x)), we get an estimated award share of .80. Historically, an award share of .80 would win the MVP.

Model Predictions

In this section I want to use the model to identify the most under- and over-predicted MVP shares in history. Remember, since this is a crude model relying mainly on leading the league in offensive categories, being under-predicted is not necessarily the same thing as receiving "too much" MVP consideration. Similarly, being over-predicted is not the same as receiving "too little" MVP consideration. But such questions can be addressed with the model's estimates.

Table 4 shows the most under-predicted MVP shares using the traditional model. That is, these are the players who received more MVP shares than the traditional model predicted for them based upon the league leaders and team finishes.

Table 4. TOP FIVE UNDER-PREDICTED MVP SHARES

PLAYER	YEAR	LEAGUE	ACTUAL RANK	AWARD SHARE	PREDICTED SHARE	PREDICTION ERROR
Roberto Clemente	1966	NL	1	.78	.00	.78
Robin Yount	1989	AL	1	.65	.00	.65
Charlie Gehringer	1937	AL	1	.98	.36	.62
Bob Elliott	1947	NL	1	.61	.00	.61
Luke Appling	1936	AL	2	.81	.23	.58

Leading the list is Roberto Clemente in 1966. Clemente won the NL MVP in a close vote over Sandy Koufax in what turned out to be Sandy's final season. Clemente had a fine year with 202 hits (3rd in league), a career-high 105 runs (4th), 31 doubles (5th), 11 triples (3rd), a career-high 29 home runs, 119 RBI (2nd), 342 total bases (2nd), and a league-leading 17 outfield assists.

This case, like the others on the list, reflect MVP voters choosing a worthy candidate who did not happen to lead the league in many offensive categories. Each of the MVP winners on the list was not an undeserving recipient. Indeed, it is in years in which there is no obvious winner that we may learn the most about what voters look for in an MVP. In short, these were years in which whoever won the MVP would be deemed "under-predicted" by the model.

Table 5 presents the five most over-predicted MVP shares using the traditional model. That is, these are the players who received less MVP shares than the traditional model predicted for them based upon the league leaders and team finishes.

Table 5. TOP FIVE OVER-PREDICTED MVP SHARES

PLAYER	YEAR	LEAGUE	ACTUAL RANK	AWARD SHARE	PREDICTED SHARE	PREDICTION ERROR
Duke Snider	1956	NL	10	.16	.79	.63
Dick Stuart	1963	AL	13	.09	.68	.59
Al Rosen	1952	AL	10	.15	.73	.58
Gus Zernial	1951	AL	20	.04	.62	.58
Hank Aaron	1960	NL	11	.16	.73	.57

Leading the list is Duke Snider in 1956. Duke led the league in home runs, on-base average, slugging percentage, and walks. Of course, the Dodgers won the pennant, too. Snider finished far down the list of MVP finishers. It seems that Duke did not receive credit for leading Brooklyn to another pennant, even with his great season, as team-mates Newcombe, Maglie, Gilliam, and Reese all finished ahead of Snider for the MVP.

Dick Stuart led the league in RBI and total bases for the seventh-place 1963 Red Sox. Teammates Radatz and Yastrzemski finished fifth and sixth for the MVP, so voters were willing to vote for players on a seventh place club. However, Stuart was not any-body's idea of an MVP so wound up far down the list. The model does not know that some players will simply never do well when it comes to the MVP.

Al Rosen led the league in RBI and total bases for the second-place 1952 Indians, the season before he won the unanimous MVP. Rosen finished 10th in the MVP, behind teammates Wynn, Lemon, and Garcia. Of course, any slight Rosen might have received in 1952 was more than made up for the next year.

Gus Zernial was another hard-luck case. Zernial led the league in home runs and RBI for the 1951 Athletics (also playing four games for the White Sox). He finished far down the MVP voting with a share of .04, one of the all-time lowest shares for any home run or RBI leader. The Athletics finished in sixth place, but teammates Ferris Fain, who won the batting title, and Eddie Joost both garnered decent votes and both fared better than Zernial.

Hank Aaron led the league in RBI and total bases for the second-place 1960 Milwaukee Braves. However, Aaron's season was seen as a disappointment following his stellar 1959 season. In addition, the Braves finished far behind the Pirates, following their previous three seasons in which they won two and a half pennants.

1998 MVPs

What does the model predict for the 1998 MVPs? Sosa (.83) easily over McGwire (.57) in the NL due largely to leading the league in RBI and making the playoffs. The phe-nomenon of the wild card really throws a wild card into the MVP deck as well. It seems that many voters are giving a lot of credit to winning the wild card, a sort of dumbing down of the voting. Since it is now considered "harder" to win the wild card (more teams are vying for it and it often goes down to the wire), the MVP may come from many wild card teams in the future.

In the AL, the model predicts Gonzalez (.79) over Belle (.68), Jeter (.65), and Williams (.61) due to leading the league in RBI.

Conclusions

In this article I have confirmed the generally held view that leading the league in RBI gives a player a leg up on the MVP award. Playing on a league or division champion is by far the second most important thing a player can do according to MVP voters. Moderately important are leading the league in slugging percentage, runs scored, total bases, and batting average.

———

This article originally appeared in the February 1999 issue of *By The Numbers*.

Linear Weights

Pete Palmer's "Linear Weights" method is used to evaluate offenses. Its formula is:

$$LW = .46(1B) + .8(2B) + 1.02(3B) + 1.4\,(HR) + .33(BB) + .3(SB) - .6(CS) - .25(AB\text{-}H)$$

LW is denominated in runs above average. If *LW* is negative, that means the player or team was below average; at zero, linear weights is saying that a batting line is exactly average.

In a sense, linear weights "competes" with Runs Created, in that both statistics evaluate offenses. Let's look again at Mark McGwire and Sammy Sosa's 1998:

	AB	H	2B	3B	HR	BB	SB	CS	AVG	LW
McGwire	509	152	21	0	70	162	1	0	.299	+107
Sosa	643	198	20	0	66	73	18	9	.308	+73

And so linear weights tells us that Mark McGwire's season is worth 107 runs above average, and Sammy Sosa's is worth 73.

You'll notice that this is very similar to how Runs Created evaluated those two seasons (page 8). If it wasn't, that would be evidence that one or the other statistic didn't work.

Introduction to "The Recipe for a Stolen Base"

It's human nature, when things happen, to wonder just *why* they happened. When a player hits a home run, how come he hit that home run at that given moment? The reasons are pretty simple: the player is a good home run hitter, the pitcher throws a juicy pitch, and the combination led to the home run.

In general, we have a pretty good idea in what relative proportions we assign blame (or credit) for the home run. We may not be able to say it in so many words, but we understand that most of the credit for the homer goes to the batter. Some blame goes to the pitcher, but less. We'd say that home runs are "mostly" due to the skill of the hitter, and "a little bit" due to that of the pitcher. This is a generality, of course.

For stolen bases, though, our intuitive sense is much less finely tuned. We understand that most of the credit belongs to the runner, but how much? Catchers vary in throwing ability, and pitchers differ in how well they are able to control the steal, either by speed of delivery or pickoff move. How much do these matter relative to each other?

It is this question that Sig Mejdal attempts to answer in this study. He won't tell us who the best stealing runners are, or the catchers with the best arms—these facts are available other places. What he does tell us is their relative importance. Is the identity of the runner twice as important as knowing who the pitcher is? Three times? Four times? Does the umpire matter at all? And what about the playing surface—is a strong catcher more important than playing on turf or less important? And how much more or less?

Read on.

PHIL BIRNBAUM

The Recipe for a Stolen Base

by Sig Mejdal

The score was 0-0 in game three of the World Series as Steve Finley stepped off first base, carefully eyeing the pitcher, David Cone, as he inched his way toward second. Meanwhile behind the plate, catcher Joe Girardi readied himself for the impending throw to second. Cone delivered as Finley broke toward second. Girardi caught, turned, and hurled the ball to second base . . . the tag was applied . . . and alas, the safe sign was given by umpire Tim Tschida.

This seemingly routine steal of second made me wonder exactly what factors led to that safe call by Tim Tschida. In other words, what influences the outcome of a stolen base?

We know that Finley is a very good base stealer. Over the last three years, he has been caught only 81 times in nearly 330 attempts—a 75% success rate. Certainly Finley's base-stealing ability had something to do with the outcome. Behind the plate is Girardi. Attached to his shoulder is a below-average throwing arm (runners stole on him at an 80% rate). It's a safe bet that he had something to do with it. Now, on the mound is David Cone. He must have had something to do with the outcome. After all, he was holding the runner on, maybe occasionally making a pickoff attempt, and it was the leg kick of his delivery that acted like the starter's pistol in this race. As if that wasn't enough, the replay revealed that Finley was actually tagged before he reached the haven of second base. Albeit a very close call, Tschida blew it. Could there be a tendency for some umpires to consistently slant their safe/out calls? Maybe Tschida "safe/out tendencies" should be thrown into the soup as well. And while we are at it, it was hard not to notice that Finley ran the whole way to second on dirt—certainly he could have got there more quickly if he had the benefit of running on artificial turf. Let's include the surface as well.

So our ingredients are baserunner, catcher, pitcher, umpire, and surface. Our goal is to find out how important each one is to the results of a stolen base attempt. The stolen base data is out there. We have (or can get) stolen base percentages for baserunners, catchers, pitchers, umpires, and surfaces. Clearly the biggest hurdle in our way to determining the correct recipe is the confounding effects between pitchers and catchers on the same team. That is, pitchers are paired with the same backstop the majority of the time, and it is difficult to separate their individual contributions. The last few Piazza years in L.A. is a good example. The Dodger pitchers were almost always paired up with Piazza. So whether he is exceptional or poor at throwing out baserunners, the Dodger hurlers' stolen base data is going to be influenced by him. Similarly, and more confounding, is the simultaneous benefit that Piazza might be getting from the staff if they were, on average, good at halting the stolen base.

It is not intuitively easy to figure out how to solve this problem. The pitcher is influenced by the catcher, but then the catcher is also influenced by the remaining staff. The goal, however, is obvious—a measure for the pitcher and a measure for the catcher that are both accurate and independent of each other's skills. As we have it now, the pitcher's SB rate is really a measure of his ability to hold the runners on, and the arms of the catchers that he has been paired up with.

One step toward a solution to this would be to look at a larger sample—say three years. During this time catchers are teamed up with so many different pitchers that it is very unlikely that they have a significantly "unbalanced" sample of good or bad pitchers. Indeed, a correction to adjust the catchers' percentage by the average pitchers' SB% that they have teamed with showed no significant change to the catchers' numbers. In general, over a three-year sample, catchers team up with so many different pitchers that their stolen base percentage is an "unconfounded" measure of their skill. Indeed, it is more accurate to say that the pitchers' data is contaminated/confounded by the catchers and not vice-versa.

Of course, to get an "independent" measure of the pitchers' skill, we must account for the catchers' influence by subtracting the catchers' "worth" from the pitchers' results. In other words, if Cone had been paired up with catchers that averaged a 60% stolen base success rate, then we would expect him to give up stolen bases at a 60% rate *if* he were completely average. Now, if he outdoes this estimate (e.g., runners steal only 40% off him), then this difference (20%) can be attributed to him. I'll call it the pitcher's stolen base value.

Thanks to the Retrosheet play-by-play data available, I was able to collect and analyze every steal of second base attempted (more than 10,000) in the three-year sample. Information on the stolen base percentages of the baserunner, catcher, and umpire, as well as the type of surface and the pitcher's stolen base value, were put into a computer. (Of course, so as not to be influenced by the results of the particular SB attempt in question, the numbers were calculated for all the other attempts in which they participated in during the three-year sample.) Got it? For instance, if Tim Raines has just attempted to steal, I have in the database his percentage for all the other attempts he has had over the three years. Similarly, the pitcher's, catcher's, and umpire's percentages for all their other attempts are also included.

If you could imagine a very long table (or spreadsheet) of numbers divided into six columns, you would see what the computer had to work with. The first four columns contain the SB percentages for the baserunner, catcher, pitcher, and umpire involved in the particular attempt. The fifth column contains information on the surface (turf or grass), and the sixth column has the result of the SB attempt (1 for safe, 0 for out). Each row in this table corresponds to a particular SB attempt in the three-year sample. Hence a table with a whopping 10,000 rows. I politely asked the computer to go through each and every row and determine what the best way to weigh the measures of the runner, catcher, pitcher, umpire and the surface were, in order to predict the outcome of the stolen base attempt as accurately as possible. By analyzing all the data, the computer can compute just how much each measure contributes to the outcome of the SB attempt. That is, we can look at the partial correlation constants and determine just what effect the baserunner, catcher, pitcher, umpire, and the surface have upon the stolen base outcome.

As in our case with the stolen base attempt result, we have multiple independent variables (baserunners', catchers', and the pitchers' skills, along with the umpires' tendency and the surface) that may influence the dependent variable (outcome of the stolen base attempt) instead of just one variable. So now we will look at a *partial correlation coefficient* instead of a correlation coefficient. The partial correlation coefficient is a measure between the dependent variable (stolen base result) and one particular independent variable when all other variables involved are kept constant; that is, when the effects of all other variables are removed (often indicated by the phrase "other things being equal"). It is the unique contribution of the particular independent variable to the prediction of the dependent variable. In other words, it is the effect that each of our "ingredients" have upon the stolen base.

The resulting listing gives the partial correlation coefficients* for each of our independent variables:

PARTIAL CORRELATION COEFFICIENTS	
BASERUNNERS SB%	.16
CATCHERS SB%	.08
PITCHERS SB VALUE	.15
UMPIRES SB%	.00
SURFACE	.05

Another way to think of these coefficients is as relative weights of contributions to the outcome. Of the variation that can be explained by this model, the table below gives a percentage breakdown for each factor:

PERCENT OF EXPLAINABLE VARIATION	
BASERUNNERS SB%	36%
CATCHERS SB%	19%
PITCHERS SB VALUE	34%
UMPIRES SB%	0%
SURFACE	11%

Not surprisingly, the baserunner has the biggest influence on the outcome. But, believe it or not, just a hair behind him is the pitcher's influence. This means that the two most important bits of information to have if we want to discover the likely outcome of a stolen base attempt are measures of the baserunner's skill and the pitcher's skill—not the catcher's skill. It is quite enlightening to discover that the catcher's arm is just slightly more than half as important as either of these effects. In fact, the surface alone is about half as influential as the catcher's arm. As you can see, the data reveal that the umpires have nothing to do with it. Sure, some umps may have made 75% safe calls while other made 65%, but these differences mean nothing—just normal deviations that come from sampling.

* You will note that I did not include the actual regression formula. This was done on purpose for a couple of reasons. First of all, the magnitude of the numbers associated with each of the "ingredients" is not the best indicator of the contributing effects of each. That is, the magnitude of the regression coefficient is influenced by the variability of the measurements themselves. I wanted to discover the relative importance of each factor, not necessarily generate a predictive formula. Second, I conducted a linear multiple regression, while a logistic multiple regression would have been more appropriate, since we have maximum and minimum allowable values (i.e., 100% and 0% predictive range for the stolen base success rate). The relative values of the partial correlation coefficients will be nearly the same; however, the linear regression equation would generate nonsense predictions (110% success rate) for some relatively extreme combinations of players. For those reasons, I left it off for now.

This article originally appeared in the August 2000 issue of *By The Numbers*.

Introduction to "Playing Every Day and September Performance"

It's 1992, you're a sabermetrician, and you decide to look at player performance through the prism of playing time. Remarkably, you discover real evidence that a certain All-Star renowned for his daily play is grossly underperforming in the last month of the season, every season. Your work, published in a widely read, very influential sabermetrics journal, results in that player being rested on a regular basis ever afterward, ending a consecutive-game streak some two years shy of the Iron Horse's mark.

Well, thank goodness *that* never happened. With a tip of the cap to St. Cal, here is Harold Brooks's article, which did appear in a very influential sabermetrics journal—fortunately, one that was not widely read!

F.X. FLINN

Playing Every Day and September Performance

by Harold Brooks

Introduction

Consider the following two players. Both play, very well, a crucial defensive position. Offensive statistics for eight years out of the heart of their careers have been averaged for 700 plate appearances, approximately what they averaged per year. Which player would you rather have on your team?

Table 1: PERFORMANCE DATA

	AB	H	2B	3B	HR	BB	K	BA	SLG	OBA
Player A	625	177	33	4	26	75	68	.283	.471	.360
Player B	636	162	31	2	24	64	69	.255	.424	.323

Clearly Player A is a better offensive performer than Player B, hitting for more power and walking more often, as well as hitting for a higher average. The only problem in the choice is the fact that these two players are actually the same man. Player A is Cal Ripken's performance from April through August in 1984-1991. Player B is Ripken in September and October for those same years. Since Ripken is the only man to play every game for all eight of those years, a logical question to ask is whether playing every day is the reason behind the late-season decline. In the specific case of Ripken, we probably can't come to a definite conclusion. Three further questions of a more general nature come up, however, that might shed light on Ripken's situation:

1. Is Ripken alone or do other everyday (or nearly everyday) players suffer a similar decline?
2. If other players decline as Ripken does, do they have anything in common other than getting very few days off?
3. Again, if other players decline as Ripken does, how much rest is required to lessen the chances of a player declining late in the season?

To evaluate these questions, I will look at players who started almost every game in a season from 1984 through 1991, using monthly data from *The Elias Baseball Analyst* and *The Great American Baseball Stat Book* from those years. The players are initially divided into three groups by number of games started. The three groups are 158-162 starts, 153-157 starts, and 148-152 starts. The measures of performance I use are batting average (BA), slugging average (SA), on-base average (OBA), and runs created per game (RC/G), using the basic formula and 25.5 batting outs per game.

In order to provide some context, we should know that, on average, overall batting performances decline in September. Over the eight-year period, major league BA, SA, OBA, and RC/G [B/S/O/R] decline by .002, .006, .002, and 0.11 respectively after the end of August. As a result of this, all of the discussion of players will consider how they performed relative to the league/season they were in.

In general, the numbers to be presented will report the mean value of the group of players meeting the criteria for games started and position played, as well as the percentage of players declining, and the percentage of players falling within the categories of RC/G. These categories are major decline (more than 2 RC/G), minor declines (between 1 and 2 RC/G), neutral (less than 1 RC/G), minor rises, and major rises.

Results

As a starting point, let's look at all players starting at least 148 games over eight years, regardless of position (see Table 2). N represents the number of players in each category, and the values in the other columns represent changes from April-August performance to September-October performance relative to the league; a negative number means that a player declined more than the league average. There is a slight tendency for players starting more games to perform worse late in the season.

Table 2.
PERFORMANCE CHANGE FOR ALL PLAYERS STARTING AT LEAST 148 GAMES, 1984-1991.

STARTS	N	BA	SA	OBA	RC/G
158-162	77	-.002	.000	-.007	-.13
153-157	100	-.001	.007	.002	.09
148-152	137	.007	.015	.008	.33
TOTAL	314	.002	.008	.002	.13

Similarly, a larger fraction, 25% of all players starting at least 158 games, suffers major declines late in the season than those with more rest. Meanwhile, those getting 10-14 games off are much more likely to improve by 2+RC/G in September than to decline (19% versus 9%) (see Table 3).

Table 3: DECLINES IN RC/G

	DECLINE			RISE	
STARTS	MAJOR	MINOR	NEUTRAL	MAJOR	MINOR
158-162	25%	14%	29%	18%	14%
153-157	19%	15%	32%	13%	21%
148-152	9%	16%	36%	20%	19%
TOTAL	16%	15%	33%	17%	18%

Segregating players by position played is also of interest. During this time period, only one catcher, Benito Santiago in 1991, started as many as 148 games in a position at catcher. Obviously, this is not a large enough sample to consider the effects of rest on performance. Similarly, there are not many first basemen in the sample. Only nine first basemen started at least 158 games. There is a suggestion that the amount of rest has little effect on first basemen's offensive performance at the end of the season, but the sample is too small to make a definite determination. As a result, two groups have been selected for further analysis. The first is the "throwing" infielders—second base, shortstop, and third base. The second is the outfield. Discussion is restricted to players making the requisite number of starts at these positions. For example, a player starting 100 games at third base and 60 games at second will not be included, but a player starting 100 at third and 60 at second will be. The results are summarized in Tables 4 through 7, which present information similar to that in Tables 2 and 3, except for "throwing" infielders (Tables 4 and 5) and for outfielders (Tables 6 and 7).

Table 4. PERFORMANCE CHANGE FOR ALL PLAYERS STARTING AT LEAST 148 GAMES
AS THROWING INFIELDERS, 1984-1991 STARTS

STARTS	N	BA	SA	OBA	RC/G
158-162	36	-.015	-.014	-.016	-.49
153-157	39	.004	.021	.010	.41
148-152	58	.003	.011	.005	.22
TOTAL	133	-.002	.007	.002	.07

Table 5. DECLINES IN RC/G, THROWING INFIELDERS

STARTS	DECLINE		NEUTRAL	RISE	
	MAJOR	MINOR		MAJOR	MINOR
158-162	28%	22%	19%	25%	6%
153-157	13%	13%	36%	15%	23%
148-152	9%	21%	34%	16%	21%
TOTAL	15%	19%	31%	18%	17%

Looking at players segregated by position, the dominant feature is the poor late-season performance of throwing infielders getting fewer than five games off. Their batting, slugging, and on-base averages all drop by approximately 0.15, on average (see Table 4). Half of them suffer a decline of more than 1 RC/G, and as a whole, the group drops by 0.49 RC/G (10% of the pre-September value). Only 2 of the 36 players have major rises in the late season (Table 5). This is in sharp contrast to the infielders getting more rest, where major rises are more common than major declines. The no-rest effect is not just due to the presence of Cal Ripken in the data set. More than 20% of the non-Ripken seasons have major declines, while only 7% have major increases. With more rest, the fraction of infielders having major offensive declines decreased. Players receiving more rest have a much greater chance of having an improved late-season performance and a much lesser chance of having a poor finish.

Table 6. PERFORMANCE CHANGE FOR ALL PLAYERS STARTING AT LEAST 148 GAMES
IN THE OUTFIELD, 1984-1991

STARTS	N	BA	SA	OBA	RC/G
158-162	16	.007	.012	-.002	16
153-157	27	-.003	-.019	-.003	-.33
148-152	43	.009	.015	.013	.45
TOTAL	86	.005	.004	.005	.15

Table 7. DECLINES IN RC/G FOR OUTFIELDERS

STARTS	DECLINE		NEUTRAL	RISE	
	MAJOR	MINOR		MAJOR	MINOR
158-162	19%	13%	31%	13%	25%
153-157	33%	7%	33%	7%	19%
148-152	9%	21%	30%	26%	14%
TOTAL	19%	15%	31%	17%	17%

The outfield group shows a somewhat different pattern, with less extreme behavior at the low-rest end of the scale. While the fraction of players declining is approximately 50% at the two lower rest intervals, 33% of the outfielders starting between 153 and 157 games suffer major declines, most of which results from a loss of .019 in SA. This is in contrast to the other two groups of outfielders and makes it difficult to reach definitive conclusions about the effects of rest on outfielder performance. By the 10-14 game rest interval, however, the fraction of outfielders declining has fallen to 43%, and 40% have at least a minor rise in September. As with infielders, the chance of a major decline has fallen. Curiously, the highest-rest class for both infielders and outfielders shows a tendency for fewer major performance changes, hinting at a possibility that more rest results in more consistent behavior.

Conclusions

Some attempts to answer the questions posed in the introduction can be made, based on the data presented above:

1. Cal Ripken is not alone in suffering declines when playing every day of the season. Indeed, everyday players seem to be more likely to decline than to improve.
2. Throwing infielders (2B, SS, 3B) appear to suffer more than other players when they play every day. Ripken declines slightly more than his counterparts, but that may be a result of his getting no days off while the group studied here included players receiving up to four days off. Interestingly, despite the adverse effect on infielders of everyday play, they are more likely to receive little rest than are outfielders (4.5 infielders per year in the majors compared to 2 outfielders).
3. As little as five days off alleviates many of the problems in September. Certainly, by 10 days off, the chances of a September offensive disaster are small.

There are some interesting implications of these results. Playing players every day increases the chances of poor late-season performance, a factor that may be critical for teams entering post-season play. Only 1-2 days off per month may be sufficient to counteract the apparent effects of fatigue. Anecdotally, Cal Ripken's best September between 1984 and 1991 was in 1985, when he received two additional days off in August because of a players' strike.

On a final note, it is possible that September declines for everyday players are a relatively recent phenomenon. The current major league baseball schedule consists of 162 games in 182 days. The players thus get 20 days off, plus the number of doubleheaders played. With the near death of the scheduled doubleheader and the decrease in the number of rainouts requiring additional doubleheaders, teams rarely get more than 25 days off in a season. This number used to be much higher. For example, the 1969 Mets had 36 days off, or more than ten days more than any team in 1991. This is approximately the number of days off that appears necessary to lessen September declines. As a result, it is possible that September declines were less frequent in the past.

(Acknowledgment: Greg Spira helped gather data for 1989 and 1990.)

This article originally appeared in the October 1992 issue of *By The Numbers*.

Introduction to
"How Often Does the Best Team Win the Pennant?"

As baseball fans we might think of a player as "lucky" on a play where something unusual occurs beyond a player's control. For instance, a ball that takes a funny hop in the infield, eluding the shortstop, who otherwise would have been in perfect position. Or a long double that would have scored the runner on first had it bounced off the top of the wall instead of over it.

But to sabermetricians, "luck" has a broader meaning. To us, a player is "lucky" if he does better than what his abilities suggest he should do, and "unlucky" if he does worse. When a player goes 3-for-4 in a game, when he's not really a .750 hitter, we will say that his performance was due mostly to luck. Many fans will rebel at this idea—after all, he did exactly what he wanted to do: slap an inside pitch over the shortstop's head, or read a curveball perfectly and line it into center field. If Barry Bonds hits three home runs in a game, how can we call that "luck" when Jose Oquendo would never do that in three lifetimes?

The answer is that Bonds' feat was a combination of luck and skill. A home run requires Barry Bonds to do many things, most of which are out of his conscious control. He has to be able to guess the pitch, instantaneously estimate where the ball will end up over the plate, and reflexively swing the bat at exactly the right millisecond. And the pitch itself was governed by similar factors over which even the pitcher had no real control.

Skilled though Barry Bonds may be, sometimes things won't go his way, and he'll go 0-for-4. Sometimes he'll hit three home runs. The factors that lead to such different outcomes we call "luck."

In Sabermetric studies, we usually treat each batter like a random number generator. If Tony Gwynn is a .333 hitter, we treat every at-bat like the roll of a die. If the die lands 1 or 2, Tony gets a hit; otherwise, he's out. To figure the chances of Gwynn getting at least 3 hits in 4 at-bats, we can compute the chance of getting at least 3 ones or twos in a toss of four dice. It turns out that after controlling for pitchers and parks, players' performances do, roughly, match those of dice. (If they didn't, simulation games such as APBA wouldn't work.)

We can extend this argument to seasons. When Gwynn goes 3-for-4, we know that he's just having a lucky game. And if a veteran .250 hitter has a season in which he hits .298, we will also suspect that he's just having a lucky year. That isn't always true, of course—he could have lifted his game to a new level. We'd have to wait until next year to see. But, more often than not, the extra hits will be a matter of luck.

Which brings us to the topic of Rob Wood's study.

Just as players can get lucky, so can teams. An average team would be expected to go 81-81. But if fortune smiles, it might have a few hits fall in at the right time, and go 87-75. Or it could get unlucky and go 74-88. Just as a fair coin might occasionally go 90 heads for 162, so could an average team.

Which all means that the team that's actually the best might not win the pennant—it could have bad luck, or one of the many other contending teams might have a run of good luck.

How often does that happen? And how often does the best team actually win the pennant?

Over to you, Rob.

PHIL BIRNBAUM

How Often Does the Best Team Win the Pennant?

by Rob Wood

Introduction

I have frequently wondered how good a job baseball does in identifying the best team in the league. After all, there is a significant amount of "luck" inherent in baseball. A line drive can be just foul by inches, a ground ball can be just barely out of the reach of a fielder, many pitches are borderline balls/strikes, etc. Countless games can go either way during a season. So, 154- or 162-game seasons may not be sufficient to ensure that the pennant winner is fully deserving.

As such, it is unclear that the best team in baseball wins the pennant each season. In contrast, I have come to believe that the best team in the league regularly wins the Super Bowl, the NBA championship, and the Stanley Cup.*

Today's degree of parity is another reason why the best team in the league may not win the pennant (or, equivalently, the pennant winner may not be the best team). From a purely statistical point of view, the closer the teams are bunched together in quality, the more likely it is that the pennant winner was not really the best team in the league.†

In this article I want to investigate these issues. I will construct a simulation which adjusts the degree of parity, and then determine the relationship between the degree of parity and the frequency of the best team winning the pennant. Finally, based on the simulation results and the observed degree of parity throughout baseball history, I will estimate how likely it was for the best team in the league to have won the pennant in different eras.††

Simulation Results

I have constructed a simple simulation of a league season. My first set of leagues has eight teams and plays 154-game schedules, each team playing the other teams 22 times each during a season, to simulate 1904–1961 baseball. Each team has an "innate" team winning percentage, drawn from a normal distribution with mean .500 and a fixed standard deviation reflecting the degree of parity associated with the league.

I use the formula presented by Bill James (originally developed by Dallas Adams, I think) to determine the winning percentage of two pitted teams. Winning Pct (A vs B) = $[A \times (1-B)]/[(A \times (1-B)) + ((1-A) \times B)]$ where A is the innate winning percentage of team A (i.e., vs.. a .500 team) and B is the innate winning percentage of team B. For example, if a .600 team is pitted against a .400 team, the .600 team is likely to win 69.2% of the games.

Using this formula, I randomly determine the outcome of every game during a 154-game season, and keep track of the overall win-loss record of each team. For each specified degree of parity in the league (i.e., the standard deviation of the normal distribution), I simulate 200,000 seasons.

The "best" team is defined to be the team with the highest innate winning percentage; ties are broken randomly if more than one team has the highest innate winning percentage. The pennant winner is the team with the most wins; again ties are broken randomly if more than one team winds up with the most wins in the league.

* These other sports pit team vs. team and therefore allow the spectator to see one team dominate another. The degree of domination can be reflected in a short series, even one game. Such does not appear to be the case in baseball, largely because baseball is a repeated pitting of batter vs. pitcher (not team vs. team).

† Parity has many benefits that probably outweigh the "downside" I am investigating here.

†† This article is an extension to an article by Bill James in the 1989 *Baseball Abstract*.

Eight Teams, 154 Games

Table 1 presents the results for the eight-team simulations. The first column of Table 1 specifies the degree of parity in the league (the standard deviation of the underlying normal population), given in terms of winning percentage. Of course, the smaller the spread, the closer the teams are in quality and the more parity is in the league.

Table 1. EIGHT-TEAM SIMULATION (154-GAME SCHEDULE)

| TEAM WPCT SPREAD | | AVERAGE | FREQUENCY BEST TEAM |
INNATE	OBSERVED	PENNANT WPCT	WINS PENNANT (%)
.000	.041	.561	12.5
.010	.045	.563	20.9
.020	.049	.569	30.0
.030	.055	.577	38.9
.040	.063	.587	46.6
.050	.071	.598	52.9
.060	.080	.610	58.3
.070	.090	.623	63.0
.080	.100	.636	66.6
.090	.110	.649	69.8
.100	.120	.662	72.3

The right side of the first column presents the average observed spread in the teams' winning percentages. Note that these figures are greater than those in the left side of the first column. There are two explanations for this phenomenon. First, in any small sample luck will play a role, where here "luck" means a normal statistical variation. Consider the first entry in the column where the observed spread is .041. In this league all teams have equal abilities (innate spread of .000). Of course, it is highly unlikely that every team in the league will go exactly 77-77. The .041 reflects the fact that some teams will win more than 77 games, and some teams less, due entirely to luck.*

Second, the way I programmed the simulation will cause the observed spread to exceed the innate spread. The innate spreads essentially are valid if the opposition always has a .500 winning percentage. However, this is not the case. For example, suppose there are two teams in the league with innate winning percentages of .600 and .400. By the Adams-James formula, we would expect the observed winning percentages of these teams to be .692 and .308 when facing each other. Thus, the observed spread will be wider than the innate spread. Accordingly, the information contained in the table may be useful for others who perform baseball simulations.†

The third column presents the average winning percentage of the pennant winners. The first row indicates that when all teams are of equal abilities, the pennant winner typically wins 86 games in a 154-game schedule (as compared to its "expected" 77). As the degree of parity decreases and the teams' abilities are more spread out, the pennant winner wins more games, ultimately winning about 102 games (out of 154) when the innate spread is .100.

The fourth column presents the percentage of times that the best team in the league turned out to win the pennant, where ties are broken randomly. The first row reflects the limiting case; here all teams are of equal abilities, so that the "best" team wins the pennant one-eighth of the time (12.5%). In this case, the outcome of each

* If all teams are of equal abilities, each game is essentially a coin-flip, so that the binomial assumptions apply. The well-known formula for the standard deviation of the proportion of successes is given by SQRT[p*(1-p)/n], where SQRT denotes the square root. At p=0.5 and n=154 games, the formula gives 0.040, as verified by the entry in the table.

† Clearly, the strength of two factors moves inversely. The impact of luck is highest when parity is greatest, and the impact of the James-Adams "log5" formulation is highest when parity is least. By running additional simulations without the log5 formula, I can estimate how much each of the two reasons contributes to the additional spread. When the true spread is .000, the "luck" factor is the sole contributor; when the true spread is .045, luck's contribution is 60% and the log5 method's contribution is 40%; when the true spread is .095, luck's contribution is 25% and the log5 method's contribution is 75%.

game is essentially a 50/50 coin flip, so that winning the pennant is due entirely to luck. As the teams' abilities are more spread out, the best team wins the pennant more often, ultimately winning over 72% of the pennants when the innate spread is .100.

Twelve Teams, 154 Games

Table 2 presents the results for a second set of simulations of leagues with 12 teams, again playing 154-game schedules, each team playing each opposing team 14 times.* The results are fairly similar to the previous table.

Table 2. TWELVE-TEAM SIMULATION (154-GAME SCHEDULE)

| TEAM WPCT SPREAD | | AVERAGE | FREQUENCY BEST TEAM |
INNATE	OBSERVED	PENNANT WPCT	WINS PENNANT (%)
.000	.041	.568	8.3
.010	.044	.571	15.3
.020	.048	.576	23.8
.030	.053	.585	32.4
.040	.060	.596	40.0
.050	.069	.608	46.7
.060	.077	.621	52.3
.070	.085	.634	57.1
.080	.095	.649	61.4
.090	.105	.663	64.8
.100	.115	.677	67.8

Actual League Data

I now want to make use of the simulation results to estimate how likely the best team won the pennant throughout baseball history. As the simulations indicated, a key determining factor is the spread in the teams' winning percentages. Accordingly, I tabulated this data in different eras during the 20th century.

Table 3 presents the actual team spreads. 1904 is the first year I looked at, as it was the first season with a 154-game schedule. The table generally presents the results by decade. I have split the "modern" era into 1961/2-1975 as the post-expansion pre–free-agency era, and 1976-99 as the post-expansion post–free-agency era.†

Recall that the degree of parity in the league is inversely related to this spread. Thus, the table indicates that the degree of parity has increased greatly over time. In the early decades of the century, the observed spread in team winning percentages was about .100 (15 games out of 154), allowing the typical pennant winner to win about 100 games (out of 154). Parity has increased until now the spread in teams' winning percentages is around .065 (10 games out of 162), allowing the typical pennant winner to win about 98 games (out of 162).

The final column comes from the previous simulation tables. For example, the first row indicates that the average pennant winner's winning percentage in 1904-09 was .660, with a typical spread in team winning percentages of .118. Looking at our first simulation table (the results for the eight-team leagues) tells us that these data are consistent with a spread among the teams' "innate" winning percentages of about .100. And in such a league, the best team can be expected to win the pennant about 72% of

* For simplicity, I do not model divisions or playoffs. I take the pennant winner to be the team with the most wins during the regular season. Relatedly, I did not simulate 162-game seasons, though the results should be similar.

† The table excludes shortened seasons such as 1918, 1994, 1995, and the first year following each league expansion. Also, the "pennant" winner is taken to be the team with the best regular season record in each league.

the time.

Generally speaking, the table tells us that about 65-70% of the time the pennant winner was likely to be the league's best team from 1904-1961/2. Several rounds of expansions lowered this to about 50% in 1961/2-75. Free agency and a couple additional rounds of expansions further lowered this percentage to about 45% today.

Table 3. Team Winning Percentage by Decade

Period	# Teams	Avg. WPCT	WPCT Spread	Implied Pct. Best Team Wins
1904-09	8	.660	.118	72
1910-19	8	.648	.100	70
1920-29	8	.627	.091	65
1930-39	8	.640	.099	68
1940-49	8	.636	.093	67
1950-61/2	8	.626	.089	65
1961/2-75	10-12	.613	.070	49
1976-99	12-16	.608	.065	46

Comparison to Bill James' Study

In the 1989 *Baseball Abstract*, Bill James presented a study very similar to this one. James performed a simulation to investigate the impact of "luck" on a team's won-loss record. He simulated 1,000 seasons of 162 games each with 12- and 14-team leagues, and each league broken into two divisions. He found that the best team in a division only won 54.6% of the division titles, a "surprisingly low" percentage. James found that the observed spread in teams' winning percentages exceeded the "true" spread, as my tables confirm. James basically had two main conclusions. First, luck plays a large role in a team's won-loss record. Second, and related, predicting division or pennant winners is a difficult task.

Due to increases in computing power, my simulations were over 200,000 seasons instead of 1,000, so we can be sure that the results are valid. In addition, my simulations are based upon a parametric distribution of team winning percentages that can easily be varied.* My results are consistent with James's article. I too find that the best team wins the pennant only about half the time in today's baseball. My tables of results according to the degree of parity in the league may be useful to other researchers. Finally, I tied my simulation results to the historical degree of parity to estimate the likelihood that the best team in a league won the pennant throughout baseball history.

* I sample from a normal distribution.

Concluding Remarks

Parity has brought with it many important benefits. Teams no longer languish in the second division for extended periods like they used to in the "good old days." Today, due to the cumulative effects of the draft, free agency, expansion, and revenue sharing, most teams can expect to compete for their division title in any given season. Recall that from 1978 to 1987, 10 different teams won the World Series, and in the past 20 seasons there have been 15 different world champs. Fans stay interested over time and deeper into seasons.

However, from a purely statistical point of view, increased parity has the negative consequence of allowing inferior teams to make the playoffs and ultimately win the pennant. Using simulation analysis and a historical review of teams' winning percentages, I estimate that the best team in the league was likely to win the pennant more than 70% at the beginning of the 20th century. The increased degree of parity exhibited in today's era has driven this percentage far lower. Today, the team with the best record in the league is less than 50% likely to be the best team in the league.

———

This article originally appeared in the May 2000 issue of *By The Numbers*.

Pythagorean Projection

Bill James' "Pythagorean Projection" predicts a team's winning percentage from its runs scored and runs allowed. The formula is:

$$\frac{\text{RUNS SCORED}^2}{\text{RUNS SCORED}^2 + \text{RUNS ALLOWED}^2} = \text{WIN PCT}$$

Take, for instance, the 2002 San Francisco Giants, who scored 783 runs and allowed 616. The Pythagorean Projection says they should be a .618 team:

$$\frac{783^2}{783^2 + 616^2} = .618$$

In fact, the Giants were .590, about four games worse than predicted. A four-game difference is pretty typical of Pythagoras' accuracy.

The difference is caused by the timing of runs. Perhaps the Giants scored many runs in blowouts, or were particularly unlucky in one-run games.

Research has shown that overshooting or undershooting a Pythagorean estimate does not necessarily repeat in subsequent seasons, suggesting that any differences are just caused by lucky (or unlucky) breaks.

An alternative to Pythagoras is just the rule of thumb that it takes 10 runs to turn a win into a loss. The Giants scored 167 more runs than they allowed, so they should have turned 16.7 losses into 16.7 wins, finishing 33 games above .500. They actually finished 29 up.

Introduction to "Winning Streaks, Losing Streaks, and Predicting Future Team Performance"

When assembling a team, the front office always keeps an eye toward predictability. What can one reasonably expect from an individual player or a group of players over the course of 162 games? Even more valuable, however, is the predictability of consistency.

Though important, collective numbers often fail to tell the whole story of a particular player's value. For instance, in 2002 John Smoltz's ERA was 3.25, an unspectacular ERA for a closer. Nevertheless, Smoltz yielded an earned run in just 16 of his 75 outings. As the manager of the Braves, which piece of information do you think is more important? Knowing that Smoltz on average yielded 3.5 runs per nine innings or knowing that 4 out of every 5 outings, Smoltz allowed no runs at all?

On any given day, any major league player can have a big day to help his team win a game. How does one anticipate such a performance? Over a season, it is easier to forecast an individual's or even a team's performance, but from one day to the next is a more complex issue. When the manager writes out the lineup card, what can he reasonably expect from that group of players on that day? That is powerful information.

How did the A's win 20 games in a row in 2002? How did they manage to get that kind of consistent performance over a three-week period? Before leaping to thank the baseball gods or even the schedule maker, read the following article.

PAUL DEPODESTA

Winning Streaks, Losing Streaks, and Predicting Future Team Performance

by Keith Karcher

There is a statistical method which, I believe, allows us to test for the streakiness of a baseball team. It is the "runs test," which is used in regression analysis to determine if there are too many or too few "runs" in the signs of the residuals. If positive (or negative) residuals tend to occur together, there will be relatively few, but relatively long, streaks of positive (or negative) residuals. On the other hand, if positive residuals tend to be followed by negative residuals, there will be relatively many short streaks of positive (or negative) residuals. The same reasoning can be applied to wins and losses. For example, we can look at the first 21 games of the Los Angeles Dodgers 1988 season, grouped by streaks:

L-WWWWW-L-W-L-WW-L-WWW-L-W-L-W-LL

The Dodgers began the year with a one-game losing streak, then won five in a row, lost one, and so on. Altogether, they won 13 times, lost 8, and had a total of 13 streaks. Now the question is this: Is 13 streaks "too many" (indicating the Dodgers tend not to have long winning or losing streaks), "too few" (indicating the Dodgers do tend to have long winning or losing streaks), or not different from the expected number of streaks, given 13 wins in 21 games? With only 21 games, we could generate every permutation of 13 wins and eight losses, then count up the number of streaks in each permutation. From these totals we could determine exactly the probability of having 13 or more streaks.

As you might imagine, when the totals get up to 161 games and 94 wins, compiling the permutations can get a bit cumbersome. In these situations we must rely on the normal approximation to the exact distribution. To do this we need to be able to calculate the mean number of streaks and the variance in the expected number of streaks. For this problem the required formulas are known—they are given in an appendix at the end of this article, along with the procedure for making a statistical test.

The following table gives, for each National League team in 1988, the team's record, the number of winning streaks, the number of losing streaks, the total number of streaks, and the expected number of streaks. The data for the number of streaks are from *The Sporting News Baseball Guide*.

Only one team had a number of streaks which is outside the normal range of variation, and that one team is the Cincinnati Reds. The Reds had 97 winning or losing streaks, whereas we would expect a team with their record to have only about 81 streaks. That indicates that the Reds were much less likely to have long winning or losing streaks than any other team in the NL.

Table 1. NUMBER OF STREAKS

TEAM	W	L	W	L	TOT	EXP
Los Angeles	94	67	39	40	79	79
Cincinnati	87	74	49	48	97	81
San Diego	83	78	41	41	82	81
San Francisco	83	79	41	40	81	82
Houston	82	80	39	39	78	82
Atlanta	54	106	37	37	74	73
New York	100	60	35	34	69	76
Pittsburgh	85	75	39	39	78	81
Montreal	81	81	39	39	78	82
Chicago	77	85	45	44	89	82
St. Louis	76	86	40	41	81	82
Philadelphia	65	96	37	38	75	79

Put together, the evidence so far indicates that baseball teams are not any more "streaky" than we would expect. Wins and losses do not seem to gather together in any manner out of the ordinary. Yet some people, like oddsmaker Danny Sheridan, seem to believe that there is something special about "three in a row" winning or losing streaks. Sheridan, in particular, recommends betting a team to win after 3 straight wins and to lose after 3 straight losses. So back to 1988 we go and this time we'll just look at the NL West. The following table shows each team in the NL West in 1988, and their records following three-game winning streaks and three-game losing streaks.

Table 2. NL WEST

TEAM	FOLLOWING 3-GAME WINNING STREAKS		FOLLOWING 3-GAME LOSING STREAKS	
	W	L	W	L
Los Angeles	19	13	9	0
Cincinnati	8	7	4	7
San Diego	12	8	9	9
San Francisco	0	10	9	11
Houston	10	11	9	6
Atlanta	0	5	16	30
TOTAL	59	53	56	63

Only two teams (L.A. and San Diego) had better winning percentages after winning three games than they did overall. However, neither of these improved winning percentages were statistically significant. Three teams had lower winning percentages after a three-game losing streak than they did overall (Cincinnati, San Diego, and San Francisco). In these three cases as well, the difference in the team's winning percentage after three losses and overall is not statistically significant. Thus, it would appear that teams are no more or less likely to win games following a three-game winning streak, and no more likely to lose a game following a three-game losing streak, than they are in any other situation. If we used Sheridan's "streak" system for betting baseball games, we would not do very well. For teams coming off winning streaks, we would win 59 bets and lose 53; for teams coming off three-game losing streaks, we would win 63 bets and lose 56. Our overall record would be 122 bets won and 109 bets lost. In order to break even, none of our losing bets could be in games in which we had to wager more than $5.50 in order to win $5.00—in other words all our losing bets would have to be in "pick-em" games. Based on all the analysis here, I believe that anyone using Sheridan's "streak" method for betting baseball games is likely to lose.

Appendix

The formulas for the mean (μ) and variance (σ^2) of the distribution of the number of win streaks are:

1. Mean (μ) number of streaks $= (2WL)/(W+L) - 1$
2. Variance (σ^2) in the number of streaks $= [2WL(2WL-W-L)]/[(W+L)(W+L-1)]$

where W is the number of wins and L is the number of losses.
    The test statistic is the random normal deviate, Z, given by

$$Z = (S - \mu \pm 0.5) / \sigma$$

where S is the number of winning or losing streaks a team actually has. We add or subtract in order to correct for continuity because we are approximating a discrete distribution by a continuous one. To test for too few streaks, add 0.5; to test for too many streaks, subtract 0.5. The value of Z obtained here is compared with critical values of Z in a table showing z-values for the normal distribution to determine the probability of a greater or lesser value.

This article originally appeared in the August 1989 issue of *By The Numbers*.

Introduction to
"A New Way of Platooning: Ground Ball/Fly Ball"

It's safe to say that ever since the sainted Bill James put sabermetrics on the map, the heart's desire of every practitioner has been to unearth some strategic insight and see it become a mainstay of the game.

One thinks immediately about James's observation in an early *Baseball Abstract* that a base stealer who failed more than 33 percent of the time was hurting his team more than helping it. At the time this was offered up, AL base stealers had been getting caught about 37 percent of the time since 1959, down from around 43 percent going back to 1920. Yet after 1983 the rate drops to an average of 33 percent, hitting a low of 30 percent in 1996. The entire style of play had not changed, as it had in 1920; a new influx of talent had not suddenly arrived, as happened in the early '60s with the elimination of segregated baseball and the addition of four new teams. So what made the difference?

Could it have been the widespread absorption of Bill James's rule of thumb? Might managers have accepted the reality of the guideline? Might players have taken fewer chances, thinking about how stats might be wielded in arbitration hearings?

We'll leave answers to those questions to collectors of oral history, writers of field-manager and player biographies, and students of the intellectual history of game strategies to decide. But while we wait for those works to emerge over the next few decades, let's start watching for Tom Hanrahan's gem of a finding to become a tired truism: there is a platoon differential in the use of hitters against pitchers who are decidedly fly-ball or ground-ball pitchers, and on the face of it, the differential is just the opposite of what you might expect.

This delicious piece of statistical analysis is in the best tradition of sabermetric mind-bending. By the time you finish reading it, you'll be hearing Tim McCarver in your imagination saying, "Now, in this situation the best hitter to send up actually isn't a slugger. . . ."

Remember, you read it here first.

F.X. FLINN

A New Way of Platooning: Ground Ball/Fly Ball

by Tom Hanrahan

Over the past century, platooning hitters has become an accepted practice. Experience has shown that right-handed batters hit better against left-handed pitchers and vice-versa. In fact, when you saw the word "platooning" you likely immediately thought of right- vs. left-handed. But is the handedness of the batter and pitcher the only way to maximize performance, or even the best? What other criteria might be important?

I researched one potential factor: How do batters who hit mostly ground balls (or flies) fare against pitchers who allow mostly flies (or grounders)? As I will show, there is a definite platoon effect at work, and the results are significant. Specifically:

- Ground ball hitters do better against fly-ball pitchers.
- Fly ball hitters do better against ground-ball pitchers.
- The effects are larger for batters who strike out often.
- The effects are larger than the standard left/right platoon difference in a few cases.

Results of a similar study were reported in the 1986 *Elias Baseball Analyst*. Although the methods used were somewhat different, the conclusions reached were very similar. I will compare the two studies at the end of this article.

Data

I used the book *Player Profiles* (by STATS, Inc.) which gave hitting breakouts for the years 1992-96. Each pitcher has a statistic called GB/FLY ratio. STATS defined ground-ball pitchers (GB-P) as those whose GB/FLY ratio (ground balls allowed to fly balls allowed) was greater than 1.50. Fly-ball pitchers (FLY-P) have GB/FLY ratios of less than 1.00. Anyone in between is classified as neutral, and not used in this study. The MLB average GB/FLY ratio was 1.30, and about 60% of all pitchers are "neutral."

Every hitter has a breakout of his performance against FLY-P and GB-P for these five years. I chose batters who had at least 300 plate appearances against both types of pitchers for this study. This gave me a set of 161 batters. Their total numbers are given in Table 1.

Table 1.

	AB	H	AVG	BB	K	HR%	OBA*	SLG	K%	RC/GB†
vs. GB-P	93113	26427	.284	9687	14529	2.5	.351	.431	14.1	5.49
vs. FLY-P	67857	18412	.271	7584	11849	3.4	.345	.450	15.7	5.53

I measured an individual batter's performance by calculating RC/G and took the difference of RC/G vs. FLY-P minus RC/G vs. GB-P. When I plotted this FLY/GB difference against the batters' percent of time they hit ground balls, I found a definite correlation; the more a batter tended to hit mostly flies, the better he was likely to hit

* OBA here is (hits+walks)/(at-bats+walks), which is slightly different than the official statistic that includes things like HBP and SF.

† RC/G is runs created per game, defined by OBA × SLG / (1-AVG) × 26, per Bill James. FLY-P allowed more home runs but fewer singles, and walked and struck out a few more. Overall effectiveness was about even. None of these findings surprised me.

against a GB-P. The data was pretty widely scattered, but much of this is just natural variation dealing with the sample sizes (300+ PA) for each batter. A stronger correlation was seen when I ran a regression using the batter's KO%. Batters who struck out often have a more pronounced effect than those who didn't whiff much. A plot of this correlation is shown in Chart 1.

Chart 1. CORRELATION OF HIGH KO/FLY BALL HITTER TO
       EFFECTIVENESS VS. GB- OR FLY-TYPE PITCHERS

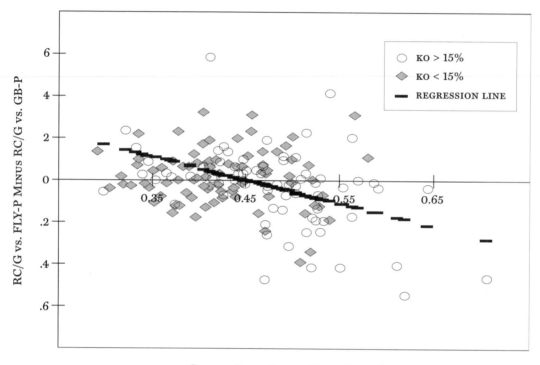

GROUND BALLS OUT OF TOTAL BALLS HIT

A linear regression was run just for the batters who struck out more than the average (KO%>15.0). The regression equation is

$$\text{FLY/GB DIFF} = -6.08 + (11.024) \times (\text{GB\%})$$

This means that a batter who hit ground balls only 40% of the time (a true FLY hitter) would be expected to be $-6.08 + 11.024 \times .40 = 1.58$ RC/G better against a GB-P than a FLY-P. A batter who hit grounders 65% of the time (a real slap hitter) would be 1.08 RC/G *worse* against a GB-P. Again, this is only for batters who strike out often.

Mark McGwire is the most extreme fly/high KO hitter in the study. He hit GB only 30% of his balls in play, by far the lowest of all 161 batters (the next lowest was 36%). He also struck out in 21% of his plate appearances. He in fact hit convincingly better against GB-P; a slugging of .721 ("only" .624 vs. FLY-P), and an OBA of .468 as opposed to .392. As Mel Allen would have said, "How about that!"

Table 2 shows the batters in the study who had the largest difference in RC/G (GB-P vs. FLY-P). The top four who hit GB-P better are all fly-hitting/high KO/big power guys. The five who hit FLY-P better are a mixed group; it surprised me that some real power hitters also hit lots of ground balls.

Table 2.

Batter	vs. GB-P		vs. FLY-P		RC/G Diff.		
	OBA	SLG	OBA	SLG	GB%	K%	FLY-GB
C Hoiles	420	613	341	395	38	19.3	-5.48
G Hill	381	578	275	424	53	22.4	-4.74
M McGwire	468	721	392	624	30	20.7	-4.65
J Conine	396	498	300	361	48	20.3	-4.16
R Palmeiro	355	499	411	620	44	12.0	3.17
E Martinez	432	539	447	671	54	12.1	3.17
E Young	318	330	404	446	60	7.5	3.28
P Kelly	241	271	351	495	46	17.6	4.16
M Piazza	356	438	424	681	59	16.4	5.84

After I found that the correlation was stronger for high K batters, I constructed a regression involving the two variables: GB% and K%. The previous regression had only used GB% and merely eliminated the low K% batters from the database. By far I saw the results most clearly when I combined the two variables into one parameter. I believe this was so because the two were related, in that many high K% hitters are also fly hitters. What I did was use the deviation from the average GB%, which was 55.3 (for the batters in this study; the actual major league average GB% was 56.5, but I think that you would get very similar results using either number), to define how far a hitter fell on the GB or FLY end of the spectrum. I multiplied this by K%^{2} (that's strikeout percentage squared) to account for how often the batter might swing and miss. By putting these together, I attempted to define how much any given batter was swinging over or under the ball. I actually used K% first, but found the fit was much better using K%^{2}. So, the best equation came out to be

$$\text{FLY/GB DIFF (RC/G)} = .078 - 264 \times (.553 - \text{GB\%}) \times (\text{K\%})^2.$$

This predicts that McGwire would hit $.078 - 264 \times (.553 - .300) \times (.207)^2 = -2.79$ RC/G worse against FLY-P. This is significantly *greater* than the expected difference when facing a right- vs. left-handed pitcher, which would be about 1.2 RC/G* (about 30 points in batting average, plus a difference in power stats). So, if you're trying to decide to bring either your left-handed flame-throwing fly-ball pitcher or your right-handed sinkerballer in to face Big Mac, I say go for the southpaw without a moment's thought. Of course, Mark is the extreme case.

Chart 2 plots the actual FLY-GB difference along with the regression formula line. You can see that the nine batters (represented by circles) farthest to the right (which are fly-ball high-K% batters) *all* hit better against GB-P, although some were very close to being even. McGwire is the circle waaaaay off to the bottom right.

You might say that there is a lot of "scatter" in the data (the R-squared value was .13, which isn't high), but if I had plotted a chart showing left/right platoon differences for 161 batters, you would see much scatter there also; it's the nature of the beast when working with 500 plate appearances or so per hitter. The student T statistic for this regression, a measure of whether this correlation might have occurred just due to plain old luck, is 5.08, putting the odds of this happening by chance at 1 in a million! I would say there is a definite relationship.

* Pete Palmer in *The Hidden Game*, p165, found that batters had an OBA+SLG of .779 when hitting with the platoon advantage, and .694 without, for a difference of 85 points, using data from 1974-77. Bill James came up with a difference of 87 points using the same methods for batters in the years 1984-87 in his 1988 Abstract. These would both equate to about 1.2 runs created per game.

Chart 2. ABILITY TO HIT FLY-P OR GB-P BY BATTERS' TENDENCY
TO HIT GROUNDERS, AND FREQUENCY OF STRIKEOUTS

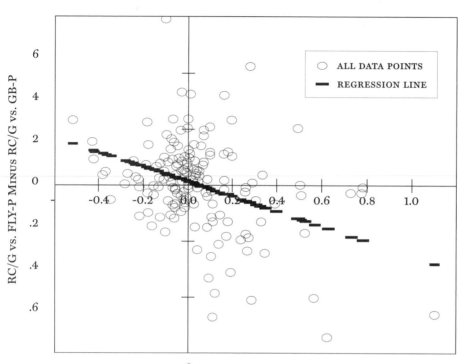

KO%^{2} × (AVG. GB% − BATTER GB%)

Interpretation

Let's step away for a minute from the data and ask *why*? I had not expected these
results, because I had always heard announcers talk about how you have to keep the
ball down to a big slugger, and how a pitcher ought to be aware of throwing a high fastball or a hanging curve to a big fly hitter, lest he deposit it in the bleachers. So, what's
going on here?

My explanation: obviously, every batter tries to hit the ball squarely. However,
power hitters tend to be fly-ball hitters, because they can be rewarded for hitting under
the ball if it goes 400 feet. Conversely, slap hitters naturally ought to err on the side of
being over the ball rather than hitting a meek fly. So, when a fly hitter swings and misses, it's often because he is *under* the ball (other times, of course, he is ahead or behind,
or takes a called strike). Counteracting this is the GB-P, who throws some kind of sink-
ing pitch that the batter tops or misses. So, a GB-P sinkerballer meets a fly hitter, and
presto, he lines it squarely for a base hit. In order for a fly hitter, especially one who
strikes out often, to hit a FLY-P with a rising fastball, he would have to adjust and say
to himself, "You know, fans normally cheer for me when I get under the ball and put it
in the upper deck, but this guy makes a living blowing the ball by (or over) people's
bats. Maybe I had better aim for the top of the ball against him." The results of this
study indicate that this mental conversation does not take place. Fly hitters do poorly
against FLY-P.

Qualifiers

While I think these findings are very significant, I should take care not to overstate their magnitude. Many pitchers are neither FLY-P nor GB-P; they are neutral when it comes to inducing grounders or flies. So, even though the effects of platooning some batters vs. GB-P and FLY-P are substantially as great as platooning vs. LHP and RHP, they apply only a portion of the time.

This study was done without looking at extremes among pitchers. *Player Profiles* did not have the data available from the pitchers' point of view. It may be that the effects are even greater for the extreme sinkerballer, or maybe not. A further study could be made using individual batter vs. pitcher matchups to test for this.

Practical Conclusions

How best to use this information? I would suggest:

- Choosing a pinch hitter against a particular pitcher.
- Choosing a day to give your utility infielder/outfielder or backup catcher a start.
- Choosing a reliever in a short (one batter or two) situation, especially when your bullpen may not have any left-handers available.
- Choosing what day to sit down your high KO/fly hitter. If McGwire ever needed a day off, I would suggest sitting him against a RH fastballer like Kerry Wood .

Comparison with the Elias Study

A study in the 1986 *Elias Analyst* used 10 seasons of data, and divided up hitters and pitchers by tendency to hit and allow ground balls versus fly balls. They grouped the top and bottom quartiles (25%) of hitters and pitchers into categories and analyzed the batting averages from play-by-play data to see if there was any difference between expected and actual bating average. The article does not explain how "expected" averages were computed, but the main point is to see the difference between ground-ball hitters and how they hit against fly-ball and ground-ball pitchers.

The Elias Study showed that ground-ball hitters batted 9 points lower than expected against ground-ball pitchers, and 4 points higher against fly-ball pitchers, for a 13-point difference. Fly-ball hitters showed an 8-point batting average difference. These numbers are about two-thirds to three-quarters the size of the right vs. left platoon differences in batting average for those seasons (14-15 points). Of course, this study only used half of all batters and half of the pitchers, whereas the platoon difference is taken for every matchup not involving switch-hitters. The Elias study used "over half a million" matchups, so the size of the study is more than three times what I had to work with in my database.

I cannot directly compare the results, since I used an estimate of runs per game instead of batting average, and also took the tendency of striking out into account. However, the results are in the same direction, and the magnitude is of the same order; somewhat less than the right/left platoon advantage for most matchups.

This article originally appeared in the February 1999 issue of *By The Numbers*.

Introduction to
"Does a Pitcher's 'Stuff' Vary from Game to Game?"

It's my considered opinion that sabermetrics is at its best when applied to articles of faith.

In baseball, it's an article of faith that some batters are "streakier" than others. It's an article of faith that for some left-handed hitters, it doesn't matter if the pitcher is a lefty or a righty. It's an article of faith that some catchers are significantly better at "working with pitchers" than other catchers. It's an article of faith that some pitchers—pitchers with similar statistics, mind you—are suitable "closers," while others can only be used as "set-up men." As if there is some genetic predisposition for one or the other. All of which is to say, the list of baseball's articles of faith is a long one.

It's also an article of faith that we—and by "we" I mean fans, broadcasters, managers, and anybody else who cares about these things—that we can, without much trouble at all, tell how a starting pitcher will fare later in the game, merely by noting what he's done *earlier* in the game. It's an article of faith that if a starter gets hammered in the first inning, it's going to be a short day for him (and probably a long one for his team). It's an article of faith that if a starter is having trouble throwing strikes in the first inning, he's going to continue to have problems with his control. It's an article of faith that if a starter hasn't allowed a hit through the first half of the game, there's a good chance that he's got "no-hit stuff," and so we might get to see something special.

This notion, that the first inning of a start has great predictive powers, can perhaps best be seen by looking at the history of the World Series. It doesn't happen quite so much anymore—probably because pitching staffs have become populated by specialists—but for a long time, if a starting pitcher ran into trouble in the first inning, he was outta there. The thinking being, of course, that giving up three or four baserunners in the first inning meant the starter didn't have his good stuff, and in a big game the manager can't afford to wait for anybody to *find* his good stuff.

Again, all of this rests on the assumption that a pitcher's "stuff" varies from game to game, that a perfectly good pitcher might begin a game without his typical stuff, and is unlikely to get it back before far too much damage is done. But of course, that's all it is: an assumption. An article of faith.

And there's a big difference between an article of faith and an article of proof. Sabermetrics is about proof, and Phil Birnbaum set out to find some proof, one way or the other, that a pitcher's stuff does vary from game to game.

ROB NEYER

Does a Pitcher's "Stuff" Vary From Game to Game?

by Phil Birnbaum

Conventional wisdom says that a pitcher's "stuff" varies from game to game. That is, an average pitcher might have his curveball breaking especially well one start, and have it not working at all five days later. By watching the pitcher warm up (assuming those warm-up pitches are the hurler's best effort), observers, and the pitcher himself, would be able to predict a good outing before the first game, and would be able to predict, before the second game, that the pitcher would struggle that day.

Do pitchers really have variable "stuff", and, if so, how large is the effect? One way to find out would be to check how much a pitcher's game records vary, against how much they would vary if there were no day-to-day variation in stuff. If, for instance, you ran random games of average pitching, you might find that quality starts happen X% of the time, while the pitcher would give up 7+ runs Y% of the time. If real-life average pitchers have both great outings and horrible outings *more* than the simulation says they should, this would be evidence of variability of stuff.

In this study I'm going to approach the question a different way. If the stuff effect does exist, you would expect that a pitcher's performance earlier in the game should allow you to predict how well he would do later in the game. In a simulation, innings are independent, so if a simulated pitcher gives up three runs in the first inning, you would still expect him to be average in the rest of the game. But if the pitcher has daily stuff, you would expect the three-run first to be evidence that the pitcher doesn't have it that day, and you'd expect him to continue his mediocrity as the game goes on.

Using data from Retrosheet, I analyzed every major league game from 1979 to 1990. First, I'll give you the batting records against every starting pitcher in that 12-year span:

	AB	H	2B	3B	HR	BB	K	AVG	RC27
Starters	539	141	25	4	13	48	81	.262	4.30

I've normalized all batting lines to 600 plate appearances, so they'll be easier to compare later. RC27 is Runs Created per Game, using the basic formula and 25.5 batting outs per game.

Here, now, is the batting line for all starting pitchers after a first inning in which they gave up at least three runs:

	AB	H	2B	3B	HR	BB	K	AVG	RC27
Starters	539	141	25	4	13	48	81	.262	4.30
3+ Runs in 1st	535	142	25	4	14	50	75	.265	4.51

First, it looks like the effect is small. Intuitively, I would have thought that a pitcher with an ERA of 27 or more in the first inning would be a disaster in the remainder of the game. But he's only .21 runs worse. If we assume this pitcher will, on average, stay in the game four more innings, it costs the team an eighth of a run to leave him in (instead of replacing him with an average pitcher).

But even that .21 runs is overstated. These pitchers give up runs in the rest of the game at the rate of 4.51, versus 4.30 for the average pitcher. But the pitchers in the sample are not average. Starters who give up three runs in the first inning are usually worse than average pitchers – the better than average pitchers do it less often, and the worse than average pitchers do it more often, which weights the sample toward the worse pitchers. To account for this effect, I calculated the RC27 of the average pitcher in the 3+ runs sample, using their season statistics and weighted by the number of plate appearances they contributed to the 3+ line. I'll rerun the above table with that added.

	AB	H	2B	3B	HR	BB	K	AVG	RC27	POP
All Starters	539	141	25	4	13	48	81	.262	4.30	4.30
3+ Runs in 1st	535	142	25	4	14	50	75	.265	4.51	4.54

The "pop" column is the season RC27 of the population of pitchers who made up that line. Those pitchers who gave up the three-run inning were, as we expected, worse than average pitchers, by 24 points of RC27. But what is now remarkable is that after giving up three runs in the first, they were *better* pitchers than their season average! Although the difference is very small, this is still the opposite of what we would have expected if there were a stuff effect.

A caveat: even if there were no stuff effect at all, we would still not expect the two columns to be identical, for several reasons:

- The three-run inning figures into the season average, but not into the 3+ batting line (since the batting line measures only what happened *after* the three-run inning). And, therefore, we would expect the 3+ line to not match the season line, but the season line with the three-run inning removed. Removing a three-run inning from a starting pitcher's line lowers his ERA by 10 to 20 points. This is quite a large difference, and would tend to hide any stuff effect.

- Just as three-run innings tend to correspond to pitchers who are worse than average, they also correspond to (a) opposing teams who are better than average, (b) games played in hitter's parks, (c) umpires with a small strike zone, and (d) any other effects (weather, wind, etc.) that would favor the hitter. This would tend to exaggerate any stuff effect.

- It is possible that pitchers do, indeed, have different stuff day-to-day, but that managers can tell, and are quick to remove a stuffless pitcher. That is, the "3+" column reflects only 3+ pitchers *that the manager chose to leave in the game*. If managers are accurate in knowing when to remove a pitcher for stuff reasons, we would expect to see a much lower stuff effect.

These factors mean that we cannot conclude, from the "3+" line, that there is no effect. However, these factors are likely small, and should not hide a large stuff effect if one exists.

I ran the same study for first innings with 4+ runs, and first innings with 5+ runs. I'll run all these results here, and I'll add one more column for the actual number of at-bats in the sample:

	AB	H	2B	3B	HR	BB	K	AVG	RC27	POP	TAB
All Starters	539	141	25	4	13	48	81	.262	4.30	4.30	1168982
3+ Runs in 1st	535	142	25	4	14	50	75	.265	4.51	4.54	34819
4+ Runs in 1st	537	143	26	4	14	50	74	.266	4.56	4.57	10657
5+ Runs in 1st	539	153	29	4	19	52	74	.284	5.58	4.67	1965

The results for the 4+ group are similar to the 3+ results: no obvious stuff effect, with the pitchers performing about as well as expected for their skill level. But at the 5+ plateau, there does seem to be an effect. After allowing five or more runs in the first inning, starters pitched almost a full run worse than their talent would suggest, giving up 5.58 runs per 9 innings instead of their usual 4.67.

But note the small sample size—the difference came from only 1,965 at-bats, or a bit more than three player-seasons. I did a quick simulation, and found that the standard deviation of RC27 is approximately:

$$\frac{17}{\sqrt{AB}}$$

For 1,965 at-bats, the SD works out to about .38, which means our difference is significant at the 95% level. But since this result may be the only significant one out of a series of tests, we should rerun the analysis on other league-years before formally concluding significance. (That is, since we have done three tests already, the chance of getting at least one at the 95% significance level is actually about 85%.)

Walks

Perhaps the non-effect for first-inning runs is partly due to the effects of luck. Even a good pitcher can allow infield hits, or bloop singles, or seeing-eye doubles. Plus, because we didn't control for unearned runs, the runs might have scored on defensive miscues.

But walks are almost completely under the control of the pitcher, and so perhaps we'll see an effect based on walks.

Here are the results for starting pitchers who allowed two or more walks in the first inning, as well as batting lines for 3+ walks and 4+ walks:

	AB	H	2B	3B	HR	BB	K	AVG	RC27	POP	TAB
2+ Walks in 1st	533	139	24	4	13	54	81	.261	4.37	4.41	54073
3+ Walks in 1st	529	141	27	4	13	57	78	.267	4.66	4.43	6695
4+ Walks in 1st	538	154	33	4	12	51	86	.286	5.24	4.51	439

As expected, all these starters gave up more walks than average after their wild first inning, because pitchers with wild innings tend to have low control to begin with. But the bad first doesn't seem to tell us much about what to expect in the remainder of the outing. After two walks, we get almost exactly a typical performance. After 3+ walks, we get a bit worse an outing than we expect, but by a very small amount. After a four-walk first, the difference is a bit more significant. We can expect a worse than average next few innings from the starter, but not by that much—less than 3/4 of a run per game. It's certainly not worth necessarily replacing the pitcher, and overworking the bullpen, just to save half a run or so in a game that you're probably losing already after all those walks.

And the result is probably just random anyway; it's only one standard deviation from expected, which is far from statistical significance. Compare the 4+ batting line to the 3+ batting line. If a player had those results respectively in consecutive years, we'd call him very consistent.

Late Innings

When a starter gets to the late innings of a game, and then starts allowing baserunners, everyone seems to agree that he's getting tired and should be replaced, before his exhausted pitching arm does even more damage. And, almost always, that pitcher is indeed replaced. But what about those times that he's left in the game? Does the expected damage materialize?

Here are batting lines for starters left in the game after allowing three baserunners (hits or walks) in the seventh, eighth, or ninth inning respectively.

	AB	H	2B	3B	HR	BB	K	AVG	RC27	POP	TAB
3 Runners in 7th	533	140	24	4	14	48	74	.263	4.35	4.07	10802
3 Runners in 8th	531	143	22	4	14	48	70	.269	4.50	4.00	3505
3 Runners in 9th	532	147	17	3	11	48	72	.276	4.37	3.89	793

We may be on to something here: whether it be in the seventh, eighth, or ninth, when a pitcher is left in after allowing three baserunners, he continues to do worse than his season average if he's left in the game. But, still, none of the differences are statistically significant.

Even in terms of baseball significance, the differences aren't much. Over the season, these pitchers are a bit better than average, which is probably part of the reason their managers let them stay in the game in these situations. Over the remainder of the game, they turn into roughly average pitchers. If the manager isn't worried about their arms, and the game isn't close, there's no reason to turn to the bullpen when you effectively still have an average pitcher out there.

Having said that, this is one result that I would expect to become statistically significant if we had more years to analyze. I suspect that pitchers do get tired in ways managers don't always recognize. But I could be wrong.

No-Hitters

If a pitcher has a no-hitter going, we'd expect that he has good stuff today, and we'd definitely expect that he will continue to pitch well in the coming innings. But it turns out that isn't the case – that he performs at almost exactly his season average after three, four, or five no-hit innings. Here are the numbers:

	AB	H	2B	3B	HR	BB	K	AVG	RC27	POP	TAB
No Hits through 3	542	136	24	3	14	47	86	.251	3.98	3.96	21485
No Hits through 4	541	132	21	3	13	48	91	.244	3.70	3.89	7355
No Hits through 5	543	134	25	3	15	46	90	.247	3.93	3.86	2748

These are good pitchers—note their above-average strikeout rates and good RC27s – and they continue to be good after a few no-hit innings. Not great—just as good as you would have expected for a typical game.

Strikeouts

Bill James has pointed out that strikeout rate is one of the largest factors in determining how a young pitcher will do in the future. Can it be used to figure how the current pitcher will do in the rest of the game?

Here are the batting lines for (a) pitchers who strike out six or more in the first three innings; (b) pitchers who strike out eight or more in the first four innings; and (c) pitchers who strike out 10 or more in the first six innings.

	AB	H	2B	3B	HR	BB	K	AVG	RC27	POP	TAB
6 Ks through 3	540	126	20	3	14	51	120	.233	3.53	3.71	6314
8 Ks through 4	534	124	18	4	12	54	136	.232	3.43	3.63	1798
10 Ks through 6	539	124	19	3	12	53	131	.230	3.35	3.47	1420

These are great pitchers—with lots of strikeouts and ERAs in the low threes. And they are, indeed, even better than that for the next few innings, but the difference is not even close to statistical significance (the top line is about one SD better than expected).

And, here, the manager's decisions do not factor in to the situation. For pitchers with a bad first inning, the manager might notice bad stuff and remove the pitcher before he has a chance to show up in our charts. But for these pitchers, the manager's decision-making is out of the picture—the only decision for the manager is to let the guy pitch, which, after 10 strikeouts through six innings, is not a tough call to make.

Conclusions

Going into this study, I expected to find reasonably hefty stuff effects. I thought that average pitchers who give up lots of walks in the first inning are showing they have no control that day, and the results would continue to be disastrous. I was expecting the RC27s to show a big jump, perhaps from 4.5 to 6.5.

But, as we have seen, they did not. There were no big effects either way, and, in general, we can conclude that there's no evidence that the results a pitcher has obtained so far in the game should affect our estimate of what we should expect later in the game.

Go figure.

This article originally appeared in the November 2000 issue of *By The Numbers*.

About the Contributors

PHIL BIRNBAUM is a native of Toronto and a Blue Jays fan from the days of Otto Velez and Joey McLaughlin. He lives now lives in Ottawa, where he works as a computer consultant and edits "By the Numbers."

CLIFFORD BLAU, CPA, is a native of White Plains, NY. Blessed with a master's degree from the University of Virginia, Mr. Blau was a 1997 winner of the Macmillan-SABR baseball research award for his article on tie games.

HAROLD BROOKS was born and raised as a third-generation Cardinal fan who got interested in math so that he could do useful things like calculate ERA. He currently does research on tornadoes and severe thunderstorms and how to evaluate weather forecasts at the National Severe Storms Laboratory in Norman, Oklahoma.

CLEM COMLY is co-chair of SABR's statistical analysis committee and a member of the board of directors of Retrosheet (www.retrosheet.org). He is a senior consultant at a small custom software company. He is a bridge Life Master.

PAUL DePODESTA is in his fifth season as the assistant GM of the Oakland Athletics. Previously, Paul spent three years with the Cleveland Indians serving as the major league advance scout and special assistant to the GM.

F. X. FLINN has been a SABR member since 1984, and the Society elected him in 2001 to the executive board and the office of Treasurer. Flinn is an information technology consultant, and lives in Quechee, Vermont

TOM HANRAHAN by vocation is an avionics systems engineer at the Naval Air Warfare Center in Maryland. He used to have other hobbies until baseball research and his family absorbed his time. By the grace of God, he is the self-proclaimed luckiest man on the face of the earth.

BILL JAMES is the author of many books about baseball, and is currently engaged as a senior adviser to the Boston Red Sox.

KEITH KARCHER has been employed as a statistician at Johnson & Johnson Pharmaceutical Research and Development since 1989.

DAN LEVITT, when not researching baseball, manages the capital markets for a national commercial real estate firm. To get outside in the summer without golf clubs, Dan plays on a 19th-century vintage baseball team that travels around the Upper Midwest. He lives in Minneapolis with his wife and two boys.

JOHN MATTHEW IV has been a member of SABR since he read the 1984 Bill James *Baseball Abstract*. He currently is living a dream as a marketing producer for MLB.com. He also shares his expertise with apostrophes in the preparation of *By The Numbers* and this publication.

SIG MEJDAL lives in Sunnyvale, California. He works as a biomathematician for NASA Ames and as a usability engineering consultant. His interests include baseball performance evaluation and modeling, along with the prediction of the outcomes of individual games.

ROB NEYER is a senior writer and baseball columnist for ESPN.com. His books include *Baseball Dynasties* (with Eddie Epstein), *Feeding the Green Monster*, and the upcoming *Rob Neyer's Big Book of Baseball Lineups*.

CHARLIE PAVITT has been involved in sabermetric research ever since discovering there was such a thing after joining SABR in 1983. The rest of the time, he is associate professor in the Department of Communication at the University of Delaware.

MAT OLKIN is a writer and copy editor for *USA Today Sports Weekly*, the author of the annual *Baseball Examiner* and a contributing author of *Baseball Prospectus*.

PETE PALMER is the co-author of *The Hidden Game of Baseball*, co-editor of *Total Baseball*, associate editor of *Who's Who in Baseball*, and contributor to *The Sporting News MLB Fact Book*. He is the creator of the statistics OPS, Linear Weights, and Total Player Rating.

MARK D. PANKIN has a Ph.D. in Mathematics from the University of Illinois, Chicago and has made presentations about mathematical models of baseball at SABR conferences. He taught math at the University of Iowa and Marshall University, and now lives in Arlington, Virginia, where he is an investment advisor.

TOM RUANE's work has appeared in *The Big Bad Baseball Annual* and *Total Baseball*, as well as in several magazines, including *The Yale Review*, *ACM*, *Carolina Quarterly* and *Witness*. He lives in Poughkeepsie, NY, where he is a liability to his recreational softball team.

RON SHANDLER, a SABR member since 1985, is the author of the *Baseball Forecaster*, now in its 17th edition. He is also the publisher of BaseballHQ.com, the fantasy baseball industry's leading premium information website.

JAYSON STARK is a baseball analyst for ESPN and a senior writer for ESPN.com. Before working at ESPN, he was a longtime baseball columnist at the *Philadelphia Inquirer*. His work also appears frequently in *Baseball America* and *ESPN* the Magazine.

ROB WOOD, a SABR member since 1987, is an economist living in Mountain View, California. His all-time favorite player is Willie Mays who starred in the first game he ever attended.

Society for American Baseball Research

Since August 1971, when sixteen "statistorians" gathered in Cooperstown to form the Society for American Baseball Research, SABR has been committed to helping people produce and publish baseball research.

Today, SABR has nearly 7,000 members worldwide. They come from all walks of life—the one thing they all have in common? A love for the game and its history.

Members receive the latest editions of SABR's research annuals, *The Baseball Research Journal* and *The National Pastime*. Also included is a subscription to *The SABR Bulletin*, special access to online newsgroups and research forums, and other special publications.

SABR membership is open to all those interested in baseball research. Annual dues are $50 US, $60 Canada and Mexico, and $65 overseas (US funds only). Student and senior discounts are also available. For details about the benefits of SABR membership, call (800) 969-SABR or visit **www.sabr.org** today!

SOCIETY FOR AMERICAN BASEBALL RESEARCH
812 HURON ROAD, CLEVELAND, OH 44115 (800)969-SABR

SABR BACK PUBLICATIONS ORDER FORM

THE BASEBALL RESEARCH JOURNAL

THE BASEBALL RESEARCH JOURNAL, the annual publication of the society, features some of the best member research. Articles range from statistical to biographical sketches, plus nearly every other topic in baseball.

- ☐ 1985 (88pp) **$6.00**
- ☐ 1987 (88pp) **$6.00**
- ☐ 1988 (88pp) **$7.00**
- ☐ 1990 (88pp) **$8.00**
- ☐ 1991 (88pp) **$8.00**
- ☐ 1992 (88pp) **$7.95**
- ☐ 1993 (112pp) **$9.95**
- ☐ 1994 (112pp) **$9.95**
- ☐ 1995 (144pp) **$9.95**
- ☐ 1996 (154pp) **$9.95**
- ☐ 1997 (144pp) **$9.95**
- ☐ 1998 (116pp) **$9.95**
- ☐ 1999 (144pp) **$12.00**
- ☐ 2000 (144pp) **$12.00**
- ☐ 2001 (136pp) **$12.00**

SABR BOOKS ON THE 19th CENTURY

- ☐ **NINETEENTH CENTURY STARS**
  Biographies of America's First Heroes, Non-Hall of Famers (1988, 144pp) **$10.00**

- ☐ **BASEBALL'S FIRST STARS**
  More biographies, includes Hall of Famers (1996, 183pp) **$14.95**

- ☐ **BASE BALL: HOW TO BECOME A PLAYER**
  1888 reprint by John Montgomery Ward (1993, 149 pp) **$9.95**

THE NATIONAL PASTIME

THE NATIONAL PASTIME features articles by members more general in nature, although some volumes are arranged in a theme, as noted below.

- ☐ **#3, 19TH CENTURY PICTORIAL**
  (Spring 1984, (88 pp) **$7.00**
- ☐ **#4,** (Spring 1985, 88 pp) **$6.00**
- ☐ **#5,** (Winter 1985, 88 pp) **$6.00**
- ☐ **#7,** (Winter 1987, 88 pp) **$6.00**
- ☐ **#10,** (Fall 1990, 88 pp) **$8.00**
- ☐ **#11,** (Fall 1991, 88 pp) **$7.95**
- ☐ **#12, THE INTERNATIONAL PASTIME**
  (Summer 1992, 96 pp) **$7.95**
- ☐ **#13,** (Summer 1993, 96 pp) **$7.95**
- ☐ **#14,** (Summer 1994, 112 pp) **$9.95**
- ☐ **#15,** (Spring 1995, 156 pp) **$9.95**
- ☐ **#16,** (Spring 1996, 144 pp) **$9.95**
- ☐ **#17,** (Spring 1997, 144 pp) **$9.95**
- ☐ **#19,** (Summer 1999, 116 pp) **$12.00**
- ☐ **#20,** (Summer 2000, 132 pp) **$12.00**
- ☐ **#21** (Summer 2001, 124 pp) **$12.00**

SABR REVIEW OF BOOKS

- ☐ **VOLUME 1** (1986) **$6.00**
- ☐ **VOLUME 2** (1987) **$6.00**
- ☐ **VOLUME 3** (1988) **$7.00**
- ☐ **VOLUME 4** (1989) **$7.00**

- ☐ **ALL-STAR BASEBALL IN CLEVELAND**
  (1997 Special Publication, 64pp) **$7.95**

- ☐ **BASEBALL FOR THE FUN OF IT**
  A pictorial about the joy of baseball (1997, 92pp) **$14.95**

- ☐ **COOPERSTOWN CORNER**
  Columns from **The Sporting News** by Lee Allen (1990, 181pp) **$10.00**

- ☐ **HOME RUNS IN THE OLD BALLPARKS**
  Listings of top 5 HR hitters in parks no longer in use (1995) **$9.95**

BIOGRAPHIES BY SABR

- ☐ **LEFTY GROVE: AMERICAN ORIGINAL**
  Bio of HOF pitcher Lefty Grove written by Jim Kaplan (2000, 315pp) **$12.95**

- ☐ **UNCLE ROBBIE**
  Bio of HOF manager Wilbert Robinson by Jack Kavanagh and Norman Macht (1999, 200pp) **$12.95**

- ☐ **ADDIE JOSS: KING OF THE PITCHERS**
  Bio of HOF pitcher Addie Joss by Scott Longert (1998, 141pp) **$14.95**

- ☐ **RUN, RABBIT, RUN**
  Tales of Walter "Rabbit" Maranville (1991, 96pp) **$9.95**

- ☐ **HOW TO DO BASEBALL RESEARCH**
  (2000, 163pp) **$16.00**

- ☐ **BASEBALL HISTORICAL REVIEW**
  Best of the 1972-74 BRJ (1981) **$6.00**

THE NEGRO LEAGUES BOOK
- ☐ Hardcover (1994, 382pp) **$49.95**
- ☐ Ltd. Edition, leather-bound, slipcase, autographed (1994, 382pp) **$149.95**

MINOR LEAGUE HISTORY JOURNAL
- ☐ **VOLUME 2** (54pp) **$6.00**
- ☐ **VOLUME 3** (72pp) **$7.00**

- ☐ **BATTING**
  F.C. Lane reprint that shares the insights of baseball legends such as Cobb, Ruth, and Hornsby. New biographical foreword and an expanded index add much to the original work (2002, 230pp) **$14.95**

- ☐ **MEMORIES OF A BALLPLAYER: BILL WERBER AND BASEBALL IN THE 1930S**
  Bill Werber is the last man alive who traveled with the '27 Yankees. His colorful anecdotes recall an era long gone (2001, 250pp) **$14.95**

NAME _____

ADDRESS _____

CITY, STATE, ZIP _____

DAYTIME PHONE _____

SEND YOUR ORDER TO: University of Nebraska Press, 233 North 8th Street, Lincoln, NE 68588-0255 or call 1-800-755-1105 weekdays from 8:00am to 5:00pm CST. You may also place orders online at http://nebraskapress.unl.edu
(11/2002)

BOOK TOTAL $ _____

SHIPPING $ _____
(Charges are $4.50 for the first book and 50 cents for each additional book)

NE RESIDENTS ADD SALES TAX $ _____

TOTAL $ _____

MASTERCARD & VISA ACCEPTED

CARD # _____

EXP. DATE _____